14-Day
Mediterranean
Diet Plan FOR BEGINNERS

14-Day Mediterranean Diet Plan FOR BEGINNERS

100 RECIPES TO KICK-START YOUR HEALTH GOALS

CHRISTINE PATORNITI, RD, CDE, MBA

ROCKRIDGE
PRESS

Interior and Cover Designer: Lisa Schreiber

Art Producer: Janice Ackerman

Editor: Daniel Edward Petrino

Photography: © 2020 Helene Dujadin. Food styling by Anna Hampton.

Cover: Easy Shrimp and Orzo Salad

ISBN: Print 978-1-64611-600-3 | eBook 978-1-64611-601-0

R0

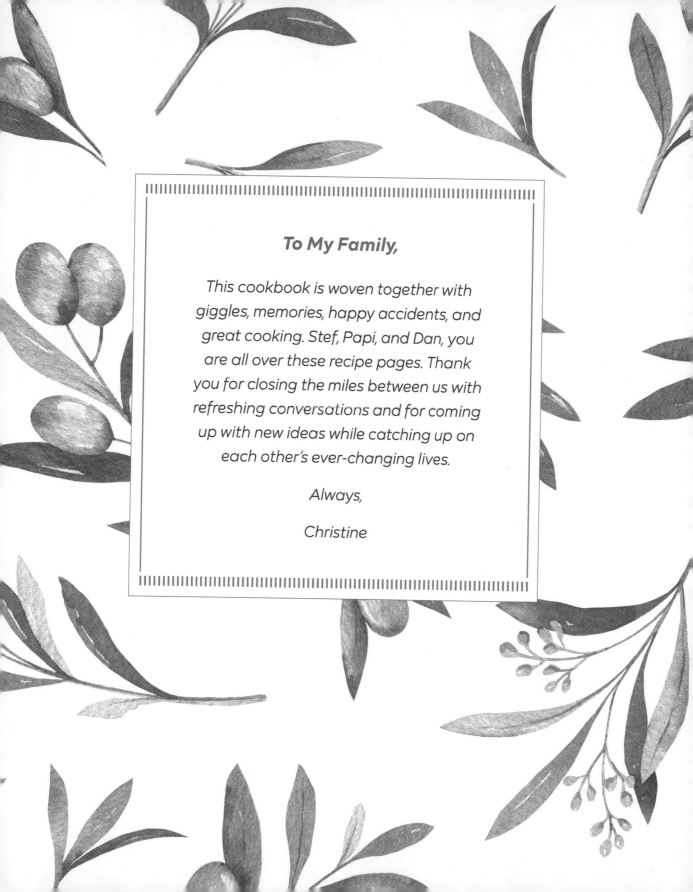

To My Family,

This cookbook is woven together with giggles, memories, happy accidents, and great cooking. Stef, Papi, and Dan, you are all over these recipe pages. Thank you for closing the miles between us with refreshing conversations and for coming up with new ideas while catching up on each other's ever-changing lives.

Always,

Christine

CONTENTS

INTRODUCTION

HELLO, AND THANK YOU for sharing your kitchen with me! This cookbook is centered on the three main Mediterranean guiding principles: using whole foods, eating what's in season, and sharing food with new and old friends. As you join me in eating the Mediterranean way and work through this cookbook, feel free to put your own spin and add your personal pizzazz to these dishes. I hope you find happiness and growth with these recipes. The best way I know to celebrate a culture is to immerse myself in their spices, flavors, and cooking habits—you can learn so much through simply cooking another culture's food. I hope you love cooking these tried-and-true dishes as much as I loved collecting, tasting, and presenting them to you.

Part

I

WELCOME TO THE
Mediterranean

WELCOME TO THE Mediterranean, a land of rich culture, food, sunshine, and a vibrant passion for life. In the pages to follow, we'll walk through your journey into the food and culture that is the Mediterranean way. Imagine olive groves spanning rolling hills and these olives being harvested and freshly pressed into olive oil, the base of much of Mediterranean cuisine. Harmony is the key to this diet; there is no single "miracle food," but rather a confluence of real foods and a lifestyle that emphasizes daily physical activity, family, community, and a slower pace. Sea life, fresh produce, citrus, and spices abound, allowing for delicious, healthy meals that aid longevity.

CHAPTER 1

Getting Acquainted with the Mediterranean Diet

THE MEDITERRANEAN LIFESTYLE encompasses a diet of fresh, whole, minimally processed foods primarily from plant sources. The health benefits of the Mediterranean lifestyle reach far beyond nutrition. In the Mediterranean, there are distinct practices of building strong communities by taking care of the young and elderly alike, discovering and living a daily sense of purpose, and intentionally practicing all of the above to decrease stress. The lifestyle also includes getting in touch with your natural surroundings through walking, visiting neighbors, and growing the herbs, fruits, and vegetables that fill the table.

SO, YOU WANT TO LIVE LIKE THE MEDITERRANEANS

Living like a Mediterranean is fun, low stress, active, and delicious! The key components of this lifestyle are a strong community and family where each person embraces their individual purpose and lives among others who love and support them. To experience the benefits of the Mediterranean lifestyle, focus on eating plants of many colors, including fruits, vegetables, whole grains, and beans/legumes, as well as consuming less meat, more fish, and more healthy fats from nuts, olives, and oils. Don't forget to enjoy these foods with a 4-ounce pour of red wine.

Mediterranean living places importance on slowing down and taking time to eat meals with good company, using the human body to move in natural ways such as walking, gardening, or using manual tools instead of modern, automated tools. It also focuses on living with a sense of purpose and belonging. Here are some basic tenets of the Mediterranean lifestyle.

EAT MORE PLANTS

Enjoy a lush rainbow of fresh fruits and vegetables and whole grains grown locally. Don't skimp on beans and legumes such as lentils and chickpeas. The vibrant colors signify a variety of vitamins and minerals that support the functions of each bodily system. The natural fiber in plants makes the stomach feel full and satisfied while regulating the digestive system.

EAT LESS MEAT

In the Mediterranean, meat is eaten as an occasional treat. Protein in the Mediterranean diet comes from plant sources and whole grains. The proximity of each Mediterranean country to the sea makes fish an important part of the diet, providing lean protein rich in omega-3 fatty acids.

ENJOY HEALTHY FATS

Olive groves dot the Mediterranean landscape, which is why this diet is rich in fresh olives and locally pressed extra-virgin olive oil. Olives and nuts are full of heart-healthy fats, especially omega-3 fatty acids. Fresh fish is another main source of beneficial fatty acids, and people who live in the Mediterranean enjoy 8 to 10 ounces of fish each week. Healthy fats also support brain function and prevent degeneration.

TAKE TIME TO ENJOY MEALS SLOWLY

In Mediterranean culture, it's important to sit down, turn off electronics, and eat a slow meal surrounded by loved ones. Mealtime is sacred and should not be rushed or filled with interruptions. Eating slowly helps the body and mind communicate in order to signal when hunger has been satisfied and before fullness has set in, promoting satiety with smaller portions of food.

DRINK RED WINE

Red wine with meals and enjoyed together with family and friends is part of the Mediterranean lifestyle, helping us unwind and connect with others. Wine should be enjoyed in moderation, typically about a 3- to 4-ounce pour one or two times a week.

MOVE NATURALLY

The Mediterranean lifestyle focuses on allowing the body to function as it's meant to: with natural movement. This means moving all parts of the body throughout the day with daily routines involving walking, active housework and yard work (with simple tools that require body mechanics, not technology), and gardening. Homes and communities are set up to encourage moving often without thinking about it. Working out in gyms and running ultra-marathons are not types of movement that are traditionally practiced.

PURPOSE AND BELONGING

The sense of having a purpose adds years to one's life span, and finding the reason to get up each morning is essential for people in the Mediterranean. Belonging to a family, friendship circle, and community enhances mental and physical health and contributes to the longevity found in the Mediterranean.

PITFALLS OF THE AMERICAN DIET

The American diet typically threatens health and longevity with high amounts of processed foods, large portion sizes, high intake of meat and low intake of plants, rushed schedules and eating on the go, and limited opportunity to move as part of the daily routine.

NOT ENOUGH WHOLE FOODS

The American diet often includes few whole foods. White, processed grains account for much of the diet, leading to high rates of diabetes, obesity, and high triglycerides. A lack of fiber and the full range of vitamins and minerals are cornerstones of American foods, which unfortunately leads to the development of diet-related chronic diseases instead of the longevity cultivated by the Mediterranean diet.

TOO MUCH RED MEAT

Red meat is higher in cholesterol and saturated fat, which can lead to heart disease. In the Mediterranean, red meat is consumed once a week or less in small portion sizes (think palm-size or a deck of cards), not a steak that fills up an entire plate. Supersized meals are all too common in America.

TOO MUCH SATURATED FAT

The American diet contains many foods high in saturated and/or trans fat, which can clog the arteries, hinder digestion, and feed the cycle of overeating. Butter, deep-fried meats, and processed desserts and snacks are high in bad fats and devoid of health benefits. Fish is rarely eaten, and when it is, it's often breaded and deep fried, removing some of the heart-healthy benefits of omega-3s.

ALWAYS IN A RUSH

The American lifestyle moves at a very fast pace where fierce competition to get ahead and constant activity lead to mindless eating. Additionally, eating is often rushed with little attention given to appetite, quantity, or quality of food. It is rare to feel truly connected to the local community or slow down to notice the gardens and neighborhood gatherings or sip a glass of wine in silence.

CHANGE YOUR FOOD, CHANGE YOUR LIFE

The health benefits of the Mediterranean diet are numerous and affect body, mind, environment, spirit, and general well-being. Following a Mediterranean lifestyle has been shown to reduce the risk of many heart-related diseases, reduce cognitive decline and dementia, decrease stress, support weight maintenance, and reduce the risk of developing many types of cancer. Many popular diets these days focus on reducing a single health risk whereas the Mediterranean lifestyle supports total body health now and protects it in the future.

DECREASED RISK OF CARDIOVASCULAR DISEASE

Those who follow a Mediterranean diet have a lower risk of developing major cardiovascular events such as stroke, myocardial infarction, or death from cardiovascular events. They also have lower LDL cholesterol due to the decreased intake of saturated fat and increased intake of healthy monounsaturated fats, primarily from olive oil and nuts, and high intake of fiber from whole grains, fruits, and vegetables.

WEIGHT MAINTENANCE OR LOSS AND LOWER RISK OF METABOLIC DISEASES

The Mediterranean diet emphasizes replacing processed grains and meats with whole foods that naturally contain fewer calories and lead to greater satiety. The diet doesn't focus on counting calories but puts emphasis on the variety, color, presentation, and attitudes about food to help manage and achieve a healthy weight and blood-sugar stability.

LOWER RISK OF CANCER

The Mediterranean diet is low in animal protein, high in plant-based food, high in fiber, and high in antioxidants, all of which help prevent cancer.

LOWER RISK OF DEMENTIA AND ALZHEIMER'S DISEASE

A diet rich in poly- and monounsaturated fatty acids and antioxidants (polyphenols, vitamins A, C, E), while also being low in saturated and trans fats, can protect the brain. Antioxidants protect against oxidative damage that can lead to neurodegeneration. The Mediterranean diet is high in fruits, vegetables, whole grains, and fish while being low in meat, providing many neurological benefits.

LOWER STRESS

The Mediterranean lifestyle focuses on routines that shed stress, such as good eating, moving, spirituality, rest, and human connection. Living in the Mediterranean doesn't mean life is stress-free; the key is managing it. Eating whole foods rich in vitamins, minerals, and antioxidants and taking time to connect with the earth, family, and community lead to a deeper sense of purpose and lower stress.

THE REGIONS AND FOODS OF THE MEDITERRANEAN

The countries making up the Mediterranean have many cultural and culinary similarities while remaining uniquely their own. Some traditional Moroccan, Tunisian, or Israeli dishes are bold and spicy, and Southern Italian and Greek dishes can be light and citrusy. Local herbs and spices shape the dishes and flavors of each region, creating a varied and exciting cuisine.

GREECE

Simple, fresh, local ingredients abound in Greece. Kebabs are made from lean, locally raised meat and served in small portions with flavorful tzatziki, onions, and tomatoes. Crunchy, feta-topped salads serve as small stand-alone meals. Moussaka, a dish of stuffed and baked eggplant, is a staple in Greek cuisine. Fresh Greek yogurt is a common breakfast, served either plain or topped with local fruits and honey. Slowing down to enjoy a meal is of paramount importance in Greek culture.

SOUTHERN ITALY

The cuisine in Southern Italy is distinct from Northern Italy. The light flavors of olive oil, tomatoes, lemons, capers, and sea salt permeate the food of Southern Italy. Each family has its own take on a caprese salad, with its base of tomatoes, basil, and olive oil. Grilled whitefish is garnished with fresh lemon slices; crusty Italian bread is served with olive oil for dipping. Meals are often finished with seasonal fruit, gelato, and small coffees.

SPAIN

Spanish lands are some of the most fertile in the world, leading to a diet full of fresh fruits and vegetables. Onions, garlic, paprika, black pepper, and green olives are the base of many dishes. Authentic Spanish tapas are small bites featuring a variety of flavors that are typically enjoyed with others. Paella is a traditional dish made with

THE BLUE ZONES

The Blue Zones Study is a fascinating investigation into the habits of people in regions around the world where people consistently live to be at least 100 years old. With National Geographic, Dan Buettner explored the world to discover the nine basic factors that were common among people in these regions, which included daily walking, a focus on family connections, and a strong sense of purpose.

Locations around the globe were identified as Blue Zones from Okinawa, Japan to Sardinia, Italy to Loma Linda, California. The residents of these Blue Zones are 10 times more likely to live to 100 than people in the United States, and the secrets lie in their interactions with the environment and the practices of their daily lives.

fresh mussels, sausage, and rice seasoned with paprika and saffron. Dairy products like yogurt and cheese are more prominent in Spain as compared to other Mediterranean countries. Light vegetable soup like gazpacho is also common.

MOROCCO

Traditional Moroccan cooking methods often employ the use of a tagine, a clay cooking pot with a lid. This vessel brings many different dishes to life, including chicken tagine, which is one of the most popular. Harira soup is hearty and comforting, filled with protein from lamb, lentils, and chickpeas, and flavor from tomatoes, coriander, and lemon. Couscous is a small, mild wheat pasta that works beautifully as the base for a variety of dishes, from meat and vegetables to raisins and cinnamon.

TUNISIA

Tunisian cuisine highlights the meeting of European-style Mediterranean with North African flair. It's typically spicy and commonly uses tabil, one of the most common spice mixes used for Tunisian food. Tabil consists of caraway, coriander, red pepper, and garlic. Each family and restaurant has its own recipes for harissa, a hot chili pepper paste made of garlic, cumin, olive oil, and dried chili peppers. Eggs are frequently mixed in with meats, breads, and traditional spices.

The Mediterranean diet food pyramid has a foundation of plants, which should be consumed daily. Plants form the largest part of the diet, starting with whole grains and followed by fruits, vegetables, and legumes, then dairy products. Olive oil is a single food that has its own section on the pyramid, which differs from the US version with notes to use fats sparingly. The pyramid moves into weekly foods such as fish and poultry, and red meat is recommended only one time per month.

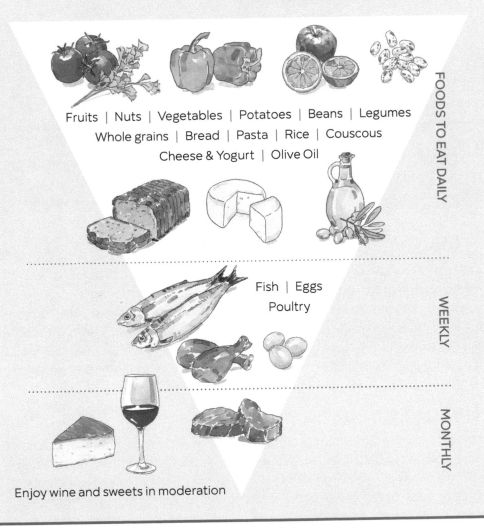

Fruits | Nuts | Vegetables | Potatoes | Beans | Legumes
Whole grains | Bread | Pasta | Rice | Couscous
Cheese & Yogurt | Olive Oil

FOODS TO EAT DAILY

Fish | Eggs
Poultry

WEEKLY

MONTHLY

Enjoy wine and sweets in moderation

ISRAEL

Hummus, a dip or spread made of ground chickpeas, olive oil, tahini (sesame seed paste), and often garlic and lemon, is a staple in Israeli cuisine. Tahini is a staple ingredient that adds richness and nuttiness to many dishes. Local ingredients come together to create dishes such as tabbouleh and Israeli salad. Small portions of shawarma, typically made from pork, beef, or lamb, are served plain or on bread.

TURKEY

Kofte, traditional Turkish meatballs, are made of beef or lamb and served with salad. Turkish meatballs are often seasoned with garlic, cumin, and paprika. Dolmas, meat, and rice-stuffed vegetables are served with different ingredients and flavors, such as grape leaves, peppers, and tomatoes, as you travel around the country. Yogurt is served with both vegetable and meat dishes. Typical Turkish dishes are not particularly spicy but rather simple and light.

REGION	STAPLES	FLAVORS
Greece	Olive oil, feta cheese, lamb, Greek yogurt, honey, pita bread, oregano	Light, citrus, herbs (especially oregano, dill), tangy sauces
Spain	Seafood, rice, onions, garlic, dairy products like yogurt and cheese	Bold, spicy, citrus
Southern Italy	Olive oil, lemon, whitefish, capers, tomatoes	Bright, basil, citrus, sea salt
Morocco	Lentils, chickpeas, lamb, coriander, couscous, cinnamon, dates, figs, almonds	Aromatic, spicy, saffron, cumin, coriander, cinnamon, ginger, ground red pepper
Tunisia	Chili peppers, cumin, garlic, couscous, lamb	Spicy, caraway, oregano
Israel	Chickpeas, fava beans, hummus, bulgur, dates, falafel, tahini	Spicy, creamy sauces made from nuts and seeds, parsley
Turkey	Eggplant, zucchini, rice, flatbreads, lamb, yogurt	Simple, light, herbs/spices (dill, mint, parsley, cinnamon, garlic, cumin, sumac)

CHAPTER 2

Preparing Your Kitchen and Pantry

FOLLOWING A MEDITERRANEAN eating style can be easy as long as you keep staple ingredients on hand. It's important to remember that this lifestyle encourages easing stress, not adding to it with complicated recipes. You'll find helpful tips on the pages to follow to make these recipes as easy as possible. The use of some Mediterranean-inspired seasoning blends is encouraged in order to keep cooking simple, save time, and maintain all the wonderful flavors found throughout the region.

STOCK UP ON THE STAPLES

There are 14 ingredients commonly used in Mediterranean eating and cooking. These ingredients are important to keep on hand due to their use across many different dishes and regions. Handy shopping tips are included here as well.

OLIVE OIL

Olive oil is the foundation of all Mediterranean food and cooking. It is absolutely essential to stock a big bottle or jar of high-quality olive oil in your pantry, as this will be your most frequently used ingredient. Olive oil production varies by country, and the range of quality is fairly large. Look for extra-virgin olive oil, which means that it's free of additives, unrefined, and not treated with heat. These aspects are key to reaping maximum health benefits. Find an oil that is actually from Italy or Greece, which requires reading the fine print, because the front packaging can be misleading. Buy in bulk to cut the cost.

VINEGAR

Vinegar is both calorie- and salt-free, but the acidic nature of vinegar makes just enough of a splash to evoke tang in a recipe. Vinegar can often be a ghost ingredient, because it doesn't stand out, but if it's missing, the dish could taste flat. Common varieties include balsamic, red wine, and white wine. When purchasing vinegar for recipes where it's a prominent ingredient, look for authentic products made in Italy or Spain using traditional brewing methods. When adding just a splash to dishes, a generic brand is usually fine.

OLIVES

Dark kalamata olives from Greece are frequently used in salads and dips. The flavor is strong, so depending on your taste preference, some recipes will not require too many. Dark- and light-green olives are mainly from Italy and Spain. When purchasing olives, pay attention to pitted versus non-pitted varieties. Unless the olives are used as a small-plate appetizer or tapas to be purposefully eaten one at a time, purchase pitted olives. Olives, like olive oil, are a good source of heart-healthy fats due to their high percentage of monounsaturated fatty acids.

SEASONAL FRUITS

One or more servings of fruit should be consumed per day, so it's important to keep many types stocked in the kitchen. Select fruits that are in season for the best flavor and nutrients. We recommend keeping some frozen and dried fruits on hand for certain recipes, especially in winter months when fewer varietals are in season. This ensures that your stock never runs out even when a grocery trip is overdue.

SEASONAL VEGETABLES

To follow the basics of the Mediterranean lifestyle, three or more servings of vegetables are recommended daily. You will find a good variety to fit the recipes of each Mediterranean region at most local grocery stores. Don't be afraid to substitute a similar vegetable in a recipe if you have trouble finding something on a particular shopping trip; the key is selecting vegetables in season when possible and choosing the freshest and best quality ingredients.

CITRUS FRUITS

Lemon (juice, zest, and slices) is one of the most common flavors used throughout the Mediterranean, especially in Italy, Greece, and Spain. The light citrus brings brightness to so many dishes. Limes and oranges are also used frequently. Plan to use a variety of citrus each week and always keep them on hand in the refrigerator produce drawer. To get the most flavor out of citrus, add a zester to your kitchen tool kit.

NUTS

Nuts are rich in heart-healthy fats and protein and are quite versatile. Use as a topping on salads, roasted vegetables, fish, and chicken or grab a small handful as a light snack. To save time, we recommend purchasing shelled nuts, whole or chopped, depending on the use each week. Nuts can be purchased in bulk to save money. The top varieties to keep on hand include roasted unsalted almonds, pistachios, and walnuts.

SUBSTITUTES FOR UNHEALTHY FOODS

There are less-healthy ingredients found in some Mediterranean dishes. The same flavor can be achieved with a few healthy alternatives.

CURED MEATS

Instead of cured meats, use nitrate-free ham and turkey deli meats.

FULL-FAT DAIRY PRODUCTS

Choose full-fat or reduced-fat yogurts and cheeses to enjoy the same flavor while ditching the unhealthy fats and extra calories you find in creams and sour cream.

WHITE BREADS AND PASTAS

Focus on whole-grain breads made from whole wheat, brown rice, millet, and quinoa. Try pastas made from lentils, quinoa, chickpeas, brown rice, and whole wheat available in most standard grocery stores.

SWEETS AND PASTRIES

Serve fruit with yogurt and lemon or a small scoop of fruit gelato. Try whole-grain toast with fresh cream cheese, ricotta cheese, or Greek yogurt and a sprinkle of cinnamon and honey instead of processed pastries.

GRAINS

Whole grains encompass the largest part of the Mediterranean food pyramid, and every region uses a few different types. Whole grains contain fiber, small amounts of protein, and B vitamins. Keep a variety in the pantry (or freezer if you buy in bulk) to maintain freshness. You will use whole grains daily as part of the Mediterranean diet. Keep whole-wheat flour, brown rice, bulgur, whole-grain couscous, and quinoa on hand. Grains are versatile and can be flavored with savory, spicy, and sweeter ingredients depending on the recipe and time of day.

FISH

In the Mediterranean, fish is consumed a couple times per week. Depending on your location and proximity to the sea, it can be appropriate to purchase fresh, frozen, or canned seafood. In landlocked states, look at the signs at the seafood counter because the labels for much of the "fresh" fish will say the fish was previously frozen. If this is the case, it can be more cost-effective to buy frozen fish and thaw it in the refrigerator yourself. Anchovies and sardines are used frequently and typically available in cans. Readily available and frequently celebrated types of seafood in this book include salmon, swordfish, tilapia, cod, and shrimp.

YOGURT

Plain yogurt is traditional in the Mediterranean. Avoid the sweetened and flavored varieties common in the dairy section. Yogurt is rich in protein, calcium, and vitamin D. Probiotics, also known as beneficial gut bacteria, occur naturally and promote healthy digestion and immunity. The larger containers are often less expensive than single-serving sizes, and both can be great staples. Use the single-serving tubs for packed lunches and keep the larger size for home cooking.

DRIED AND CANNED LEGUMES AND BEANS

Lentils, chickpeas, and fava beans are the most commonly used legumes in the Mediterranean. Lentils are best purchased dried and come in a variety of colors. Beans come dried and canned, with canned varieties saving time in the kitchen. Look for cans with "no salt added" on the labels. Legumes are a good source of fiber, plant protein, and iron as well as other vitamins and minerals.

SPICES

Most households in the Mediterranean grow their own herbs or share with nearby neighbors. If you have a garden outside or indoor pots, you can easily grow your own, but this is not required. Dried herbs are also great and, though not as fresh, still provide the same flavors with more ease and less stress. Always keep oregano, basil, chili, cumin, parsley, and garlic on hand in the spice cabinet.

ZA'ATAR SEASONING BLEND

This is a shortcut seasoning blend for old family recipes common in Israel. It can be purchased ready-made. It is a combination of spicy and citrus and evokes all the wonderful savory flavors of Indian cuisine. Thyme, marjoram, and oregano are the main flavors. Za'atar is great to spruce up steamed vegetables or add to yogurt to make a quick dip for bread, crudités, or meat.

SHAWARMA SEASONING

This should be a new staple in your pantry. Just a sprinkle evokes the aromas of Mediterranean shawarma stands popular in many countries right in your kitchen. Cumin, cinnamon, paprika, freshly ground black pepper, and more meld together, delighting the taste buds. Throw some leftover vegetables and sliced chicken into a whole-wheat pita sprinkled with shawarma seasoning, and you've made a gourmet lunch. Look for salt-free varieties to get a burst of flavor without the sodium or try the Shawarma Spice Rub (page 162) recipe in this book to make your own.

CHAPTER 3

Mediterranean Meal Planning

MEAL PLANNING CAN seem like an insurmountable task if you're new to it, especially for an entire week's worth of meals. But like any skill, you can master it with practice. There's no rule book for how to start your meal-planning journey, so it's good to ease into by prepping one or two weekday breakfasts, lunches, or dinners. Consider starting by prepping for the meal you're most likely to skip.

MEAL-PLANNING BASICS

The best advice for cooks who are new to meal planning is to stick with it! Once you establish a routine, all the pieces to meal planning will begin to fall into place. For starters, take your schedule out and look at the week ahead of you. Try and pick one day next week when you'll meal plan one to two recipes (to start) and write out their grocery lists, then pick a different day to do all the food shopping and prepping. As you continue to trial-and-error your way to meal-planning perfection, you'll find that knowing yourself and your limits will be your guiding light through this new endeavor.

LOOK FOR SHORTCUTS

Life can get ahead of us, and when that happens, eating a healthy dinner drops in priority. Take advantage of your grocery store's precut produce. If they don't have fresh in stock, check the freezer section for a variety of different vegetable cuts and mixes.

PLAN MEALS YOU LOVE

It's hard to make a dissatisfying meal when it's filled with flavors and ingredients you love. If there's a recipe you're particularly fond of, use it as an entry point into meal planning. You already know how long your favorite recipes take, so there's even less guesswork.

BATCH COOK AND FREEZE MEALS

Batch cooking and freezing meals has saved many families from drive-thru food many times. Batch cooking (making large amounts of meals to freeze) is best done when you have time to focus on the cooking process. For your first freezer meal, try something easy to make that tastes great reheated, like the Vegetarian Chili (page 68).

USE WHAT YOU'VE GOT!

When I'm particularly lazy, crunched for time, or budget conscious, I'll go through our pantry, refrigerator, and freezer to figure out a meal. A few simple, whole, well-seasoned ingredients can go a long way to making something hearty and delicious that the entire family will love.

SERVING SIZES FOR COMMON FOODS

It can be helpful—and eye-opening—to be aware of the portions you eat. Here are some serving size guidelines to follow:

EQUIVALENT		FOOD	CALORIES
Fist	¾ cup	Rice	150
		Pasta	150
		Potatoes	150
Palm	4 ounces	Lean meat	160
		Fish	160
		Poultry	160
Handful	1 ounce	Nuts	170
		Raisins	85
Thumb	1 ounce	Peanut butter	170
		Hard cheese	100

THE BALANCED PLATE

In the Mediterranean, plates are rich in antioxidants, vitamins, minerals, and fresh fruits and vegetables. A typical plate will have at least 1 cup of vegetables (fresh, grilled, or roasted), 4 ounces of protein like seafood or quinoa, and high-quality carbohydrates like beans or nuts. Red meat should be enjoyed only occasionally. Red wine is a staple in this diet, but portion control is a must at 4 ounces per pour. One 3- to 4-ounce pour of red wine is typically enjoyed one or two times a week.

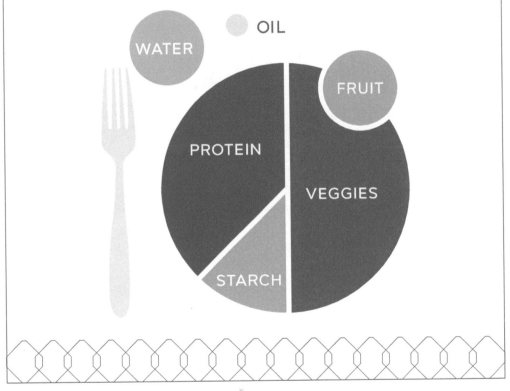

WEEK 1

This first week is about letting easy, fresh ingredients shine. All meals in the first week will take 45 minutes or less from start to finish. You'll see the ingredients used in these dishes woven throughout the recipes in this cookbook.

WEEK 1 MEAL PLAN

DAY	BREAKFAST	LUNCH	DINNER
1	Zummo Meso Mini Frittatas (page 46)	Herby Tomato Soup (page 61)	Freekeh, Chickpea, and Herb Salad (page 95)
2	C+C Overnight Oats (page 48)	Artichoke and Broccoli Toss (page 63)	Shrimp over Black Bean Linguine (page 108)
3	Zummo Meso Mini Frittatas (leftover)	Herby Tomato Soup (leftover)	Freekeh, Chickpea, and Herb Salad (page 95)
4	South of the Coast Sweet Potato Toast (page 44)	Spring Mix with Fig and Citrus Dressing (page 66)	Cod à la Romana (page 120)
5	Sunshine Overnight Oats (page 49)	Spanish Potato Salad (page 57)	Creamy Chickpea Sauce with Whole-Wheat Fusilli (page 98)
6	South of the Coast Sweet Potato Toast (leftover)	Artichoke and Broccoli Toss (leftover)	Salmon Patties à la Puttanesca (page 126)
7	Spinach Pie (page 50)	Spanish Potato Salad (leftover)	Creamy Chickpea Sauce with Whole-Wheat Fusilli (leftover)

Suggested Snacks and Sides: Turmeric-Spiced Crunchy Chickpeas (page 82), Mediterranean Trail Mix (page 77), Crispy Garlic Oven Potatoes (page 84)

PREP AHEAD

Chop the onions, bell pepper, and asparagus the night before you make the Zummo Meso Mini Frittatas to make prep time quick in the morning.

Cook the Freekeh, Chickpea, and Herb Salad a day or two in advance and store in an airtight container in the refrigerator until ready to use.

Make the C+C Overnight Oats and Sunshine Overnight Oats the night before serving for easy breakfasts during the week.

Make the Spanish Potato Salad a day before serving to allow the flavors to combine.

WEEK 1 SHOPPING LIST

Canned and Bottled Items

- ☐ Almond milk, vanilla, unsweetened (not Silk brand) (10 ounces)
- ☐ Artichoke hearts, oil-packed, 2 (15-ounce) cans
- ☐ Chickpeas, 2 (16-ounce) cans
- ☐ Fig jam, 1 (8-ounce) jar
- ☐ Kalamata olives, pitted, halved, 1 (9.5-ounce) jar
- ☐ Pesto, 1 (8-ounce) jar
- ☐ Plum tomatoes, whole or diced, 1 (14.5-ounce) can
- ☐ Spanish olives, 1 (8-ounce) jar
- ☐ Sun-dried tomatoes, 1 (8-ounce) jar
- ☐ Vegetable stock (8 ounces)

Dairy and Eggs

- ☐ Asiago cheese, shredded (1 ounce)
- ☐ Eggs, large (2 dozen)
- ☐ Feta cheese, crumbled (3 ounces)
- ☐ Goat cheese, crumbled (1½ ounces)
- ☐ Greek yogurt, full-fat, plain, unsweetened (16 ounces)
- ☐ Milk, 1 percent (4 ounces)
- ☐ Mozzarella cheese, low-moisture, part-skim, shredded (2 ounces)
- ☐ Parmesan cheese, grated (5 ounces)

Frozen Foods

- ☐ Mixed vegetables, peas and carrots (1 cup)

- ☐ Puff pastry dough, organic, if available, 1 (17.5-ounce) package, 2 sheets
- ☐ Spinach (1 pound)

Meat and Seafood

- ☐ Cod, fillets, thick (1 pound)
- ☐ Prosciutto, slices (6)
- ☐ Salmon, fillet (4 ounces)
- ☐ Shrimp, peeled and deveined (1 pound)

Pantry

- ☐ Almonds, sliced
- ☐ Balsamic glaze
- ☐ Black bean spaghetti or linguine (1 pound)
- ☐ Black pepper, ground
- ☐ Cardamom, ground
- ☐ Chia seeds
- ☐ Cinnamon, ground
- ☐ Cloves, ground
- ☐ Cumin seeds
- ☐ Dijon mustard
- ☐ Dill, dried
- ☐ Freekeh (⅓ cup)
- ☐ Fusilli noodles, whole grain (1 cup)
- ☐ Garlic powder
- ☐ Garlic salt
- ☐ Honey
- ☐ Mayonnaise, light
- ☐ Mustard seed, ground

- ☐ Nonstick cooking spray
- ☐ Nutmeg, ground
- ☐ Oats, rolled
- ☐ Oil, olive, extra-virgin
- ☐ Oregano, dried
- ☐ Panko bread crumbs
- ☐ Paprika
- ☐ Parsley, dried
- ☐ Red pepper flakes
- ☐ Salt
- ☐ Simple sugar liquid sweetener
- ☐ Turmeric

Produce

- ☐ Arugula (1 cup)
- ☐ Asparagus (1 bunch)
- ☐ Basil, sweet (2 bunches)
- ☐ Beet, small (1)
- ☐ Bell pepper, red (1)
- ☐ Broccoli slaw, 1 (12-ounce) bag

- ☐ Celery, stalks (4)
- ☐ Garlic (1 head)
- ☐ Lemons, large (5)
- ☐ Mint (1 bunch)
- ☐ Onions, yellow (3)
- ☐ Onion, red (1)
- ☐ Parsley (1 bunch)
- ☐ Potatoes, red (7)
- ☐ Potatoes, russet, large (4)
- ☐ Raspberries (1 pint)
- ☐ Scallions (2 bunches)
- ☐ Shallots (1)
- ☐ Spinach (1 cup)
- ☐ Spring mix salad greens (4 cups)
- ☐ Sweet potato, large (2)
- ☐ Tomatoes, heirloom (3)
- ☐ Tomatoes, plum (2)

Other

- ☐ Dry white wine (8 ounces)

WEEK 2

You've made it to week 2! Don't get overwhelmed by the next slate of meals as they're just suggestions. There's no law against having that delicious spinach pie every single morning this week.

WEEK 2 MEAL PLAN

DAY	BREAKFAST	LUNCH	DINNER
8	Spinach Pie (leftover)	Lentil Burgers (page 104)	Linguine and Brussels Sprouts (page 100)
9	Sunshine Overnight Oats (page 49)	No-Mayo Florence Tuna Salad (page 62)	Lentil Burgers (page 104)
10	Almond Flour Pancakes with Berry and Honey Compote (page 52)	Lentil Burgers (page 104)	Pesto and Roasted Pepper Pizza (page 102)
11	C+C Overnight Oats (page 48)	Kate's Warm Mediterranean Farro Bowl (page 96)	Falafel Bites (page 92) over mixed greens and side of pita
12	Shakshuka Bake (page 41)	Pesto and Roasted Pepper Pizza (leftover)	Mushroom and Potato Stew (page 64)
13	Almond Flour Pancakes with Berry and Honey Compote (leftover)	Falafel Bites (leftover) over mixed greens and side of pita	Spicy Trout Over Sautéed Mediterranean Salad (page 114)
14	Homemade Pumpkin Parfait (page 40)	Mushroom and Potato Stew (leftover)	Lemon Orzo Chicken Soup (page 56)

Suggested Snacks and Sides: Savory Mediterranean Popcorn (page 78), Easy Italian Roasted Vegetables (page 73), Garlic-Lemon Hummus (page 76)

PREP AHEAD

Cook the lentils for the Lentil Burgers a day or two in advance.

Make the C+C Overnight Oats and Sunshine Overnight Oats the night before serving for easy breakfasts during the week.

Chop the shallots and bell peppers for the Shakshuka Bake up to a couple days in advance so they are ready to go in the morning.

WEEK 2 SHOPPING LIST

Canned and Bottled Items

- ☐ Almond milk, vanilla, unsweetened (not Silk brand) (6 ounces)
- ☐ Artichoke hearts, 1 (6-ounce) jar
- ☐ Cannellini beans, 1 (15-ounce) can
- ☐ Chicken stock, low-sodium, 3 (32-ounce) cartons
- ☐ Chickpeas, 2 (15-ounce) cans
- ☐ Kalamata olives, pitted, 1 (9-ounce) jar
- ☐ Pesto, 1 (8-ounce) jar
- ☐ Pumpkin puree, pure, 1 (16-ounce) jar
- ☐ Roasted red peppers, 1 (6-ounce) jar
- ☐ Sun-dried tomatoes, 1 (8-ounce) jar
- ☐ Tomatoes, diced, 2 (14.5-ounce) cans
- ☐ Tuna, water-packed, 2 (5-ounce) cans
- ☐ Vegetable broth, 1 (32-ounce) carton

Dairy and Eggs

- ☐ Eggs (1 dozen)
- ☐ Feta cheese, crumbled (8 ounces)
- ☐ Greek yogurt, full-fat, plain, unsweetened, 1 (32-ounce) container
- ☐ Milk, skim (10 ounces)
- ☐ Mozzarella, fresh (10 ounces)
- ☐ Parmesan cheese, grated (2 ounces)

Meat and Seafood

- ☐ Chicken breast, cooked (2 cups)
- ☐ Rainbow trout fillets (2 pounds)

Pantry

- ☐ Baking soda
- ☐ Balsamic reduction
- ☐ Bay leaf
- ☐ Black pepper, ground
- ☐ Cardamom, ground
- ☐ Cilantro, dried
- ☐ Cinnamon, ground
- ☐ Cloves, ground
- ☐ Cumin, ground
- ☐ Farro (1 cup)
- ☐ Flour, all-purpose
- ☐ Flour, all-purpose, gluten-free
- ☐ Flour, almond
- ☐ Garlic powder
- ☐ Honey
- ☐ Lentils, green
- ☐ Linguine, whole-wheat (8 ounces)
- ☐ Miso, white
- ☐ Nutmeg, ground
- ☐ Oats, rolled
- ☐ Oregano, dried
- ☐ Orzo pasta (8 ounces)
- ☐ Paprika
- ☐ Parsley, dried
- ☐ Pumpkin pie spice
- ☐ Sugar, granulated

- ☐ Turmeric
- ☐ Vegetable bouillon
- ☐ White pepper, ground
- ☐ Yeast, dry

Produce

- ☐ Asparagus (1 pound)
- ☐ Banana (1)
- ☐ Basil, fresh (1 bunch)
- ☐ Bell peppers, red (2)
- ☐ Brussels sprouts (8 ounces)
- ☐ Carrot, large (3)
- ☐ Celery, stalk (3)
- ☐ Cilantro, fresh (1 bunch)
- ☐ Garlic cloves (1 head)
- ☐ Lemons (6)
- ☐ Lime (2)
- ☐ Mushrooms (5 ounces)
- ☐ Mushrooms, cremini (6 ounces)

- ☐ Onion, red (1)
- ☐ Onion, sweet (1)
- ☐ Onion, yellow (2)
- ☐ Orange (1)
- ☐ Potato, golden, medium (4)
- ☐ Potato, large (1)
- ☐ Potato, russet, large (1)
- ☐ Raspberries (1 pint)
- ☐ Spring mix salad greens (8 cups)
- ☐ Scallions (1 bunch)
- ☐ Shallots (4)
- ☐ Tomatoes, Roma (2)
- ☐ Zucchini, large (1)

Other

- ☐ Falafel mix, 1 (10-ounce) box
- ☐ Granola, honey (1 cup)
- ☐ Pita bread (2 pieces)
- ☐ White wine, dry (8 ounces)

BEYOND THE SECOND WEEK: EATING HEALTHY FOR LIFE

Congratulations! You just meal prepped for half of the month. Meal-planning perfection depends on what works for you and your schedule. Some may choose to plan recipes and shopping lists one day followed by purchasing and prepping items the next. Others may want to do everything on the same day. Some weeks you may plan only one meal, and other weeks you might find yourself planning two or three. Do what works for you using the blank lists below. Planning your meals helps you and your family eat healthier, save money, and reduce food waste.

BLANK MEAL-PLAN SHEET

DAY	BREAKFAST	LUNCH	DINNER
1			
2			
3			
4			
5			
6			
7			

BLANK SHOPPING LIST

Canned and Bottled Items

- [ ] _____
- [ ] _____
- [ ] _____
- [ ] _____
- [ ] _____
- [ ] _____
- [ ] _____
- [ ] _____
- [ ] _____
- [ ] _____
- [ ] _____

Meat and Seafood

- [ ] _____
- [ ] _____
- [ ] _____
- [ ] _____
- [ ] _____
- [ ] _____
- [ ] _____
- [ ] _____
- [ ] _____
- [ ] _____
- [ ] _____

Dairy and Eggs

- [ ] _____
- [ ] _____
- [ ] _____
- [ ] _____
- [ ] _____
- [ ] _____
- [ ] _____
- [ ] _____
- [ ] _____
- [ ] _____
- [ ] _____

Pantry

- [ ] _____
- [ ] _____
- [ ] _____
- [ ] _____
- [ ] _____
- [ ] _____
- [ ] _____
- [ ] _____
- [ ] _____
- [ ] _____
- [ ] _____

Part

II

THE
Recipes

NOW THAT YOU'VE had an introduction to the food, flavors, and lifestyle of the Mediterranean region, it's time to get cooking! Part II is full of delicious recipes that encompass a wide range of foods inspired by Mediterranean cuisine, many of which are staples on my family's dinner table.

Shakshuka Bake, page 41

Breakfast

Homemade Pumpkin Parfait

VEGETARIAN

SERVES 4

PREP TIME:
5 minutes,
plus 2 hours
refrigeration

When I started meal planning, I started with this parfait. The longer the pumpkin mix sits with the spices, the stronger the contrast that develops between it and the tart, plain Greek yogurt. The crunch comes from the granola, but be careful as this ingredient can pack in the hidden sugar. My trick when trying to cut sugar is to kick up the flavor. I lean heavily on cinnamon, cardamom, or pumpkin spice in low-sugar breakfasts and desserts.

1 (15-ounce) can pure
pumpkin puree

4 teaspoons honey,
additional to taste

1 teaspoon pumpkin
pie spice

¼ teaspoon
ground cinnamon

2 cups plain, unsweetened,
full-fat Greek yogurt

1 cup honey granola

1. In a large bowl, mix the pumpkin puree, honey, pumpkin pie spice, and cinnamon. Cover and refrigerate for at least 2 hours.
2. To make the parfaits, in each cup, pour ¼ cup pumpkin mix, ¼ cup yogurt and ¼ cup granola. Repeat Greek yogurt and pumpkin layers and top with honey granola.

PREP TIP: *Because the pumpkin mix can last in the refrigerator, it's great to make ahead. It can be stored in an airtight container for up to 5 days.*

VARIATION TIP: *To make this recipe gluten-free, use a gluten-free honey granola.*

Per Serving Calories: 264; Protein: 15g; Total Carbohydrates: 35g; Sugars: 20g; Fiber: 6g; Total Fat: 9g; Saturated Fat: 3g; Cholesterol: 16mg; Sodium: 90mg

Shakshuka Bake

30 MINUTES OR LESS, DAIRY-FREE, GLUTEN-FREE, ONE PAN, VEGETARIAN

SERVES 4

PREP TIME:
5 minutes

COOK TIME:
20 minutes

I have the sweetest memories of making this with my grandmother. She'd let me dice the veggies once I was old enough. With a couple of updates, I've been able to cut out some prep steps and enjoy this dish more often because of it.

2 tablespoons extra-virgin olive oil

1 cup chopped shallots

1 cup chopped red bell peppers

1 cup finely diced potato

1 teaspoon garlic powder

1 (14.5-ounce) can diced tomatoes, drained

¼ teaspoon turmeric

¼ teaspoon paprika

¼ teaspoon ground cardamom

4 large eggs

¼ cup chopped fresh cilantro

1. Preheat the oven to 350°F.
2. In an oven-safe sauté pan or skillet, heat the olive oil over medium-high heat and sauté the shallots, stirring occasionally, for about 3 minutes, until fragrant. Add the bell peppers, potato, and garlic powder. Cook, uncovered, for 10 minutes, stirring every 2 minutes.
3. Add the tomatoes, turmeric, paprika, and cardamom to the skillet and mix well. Once bubbly, remove from heat and crack the eggs into the skillet so the yolks are facing up.
4. Put the skillet in the oven and cook for an additional 5 to 10 minutes, until eggs are cooked to your preference. Garnish with the cilantro and serve.

VARIATION TIP: *For a spicy shakshuka, add ¼ teaspoon red pepper flakes while heating up the diced tomatoes.*

Per Serving Calories: 224; Protein: 9g; Total Carbohydrates: 20g; Sugars: 7g; Fiber: 3g; Total Fat: 12g; Saturated Fat: 3g; Cholesterol: 186mg; Sodium: 278mg

Morning Glory Muffins

30 MINUTES OR LESS, VEGETARIAN

MAKES 12

PREP TIME:
5 minutes

COOK TIME:
15 minutes

These muffins are a nice disruption to the myriad humdrum breakfasts out there. This dish has everything I need for a great breakfast: it's sweet, savory, and portable.

Nonstick cooking spray

1½ cups granulated sugar

½ cup brown sugar

¾ cup all-purpose flour

2 teaspoons pumpkin pie spice

1 teaspoon baking soda

¼ teaspoon salt

Pinch nutmeg

3 mashed bananas

1 (15-ounce) can pure pumpkin puree

½ cup plain, unsweetened, full-fat yogurt

½ cup (1 stick) butter, melted

2 large egg whites

1. Preheat the oven to 350°F. Spray a muffin tin with cooking spray.
2. In a large bowl, mix the sugars, flour, pumpkin pie spice, baking soda, salt, and nutmeg. In a separate bowl, mix the bananas, pumpkin puree, yogurt, and butter. Slowly mix the wet ingredients into the dry ingredients.
3. In a large glass bowl, using a mixer on high, whip the egg whites until stiff and fold them into the batter.
4. Pour the batter into a muffin tin, filling each cup halfway. Bake for 15 minutes, or until a fork inserted in the center comes out clean.

LEFTOVER TIP: *These make a great weekday breakfast on the go. Store them in individual bags for portion control, or toast and butter one if you have the 5 minutes to spare. They last 3 to 5 days in an airtight container.*

Per Serving Calories: 259; Protein: 3g; Total Carbohydrates: 49g; Sugars: 36g; Fiber: 3g; Total Fat: 8g; Saturated Fat: 5g; Cholesterol: 22mg; Sodium: 226mg

C+C French Toast

SERVES 6

PREP TIME:
5 minutes

COOK TIME:
15 minutes

This dish is as decadent as it sounds, but I'm always surprised at the easy cleanup. The marinade for this French toast gets a nice lift from the orange zest, cardamom, and cinnamon.

- **1 cup whole milk**
- **3 large eggs**
- **2 teaspoons grated orange zest**
- **1 teaspoon vanilla extract**
- **⅛ teaspoon ground cardamom**
- **⅛ teaspoon ground cinnamon**
- **1 loaf of boule bread, sliced 1 inch thick (gluten-free preferred)**
- **1 banana, sliced**
- **¼ cup Berry and Honey Compote (page 189)**

1. Heat a large nonstick sauté pan or skillet over medium-high heat.
2. In a large, shallow dish, mix the milk, eggs, orange zest, vanilla, cardamom, and cinnamon. Working in batches, dredge the bread slices in the egg mixture and put in the hot pan.
3. Cook for 5 minutes on each side, until golden brown. Serve, topped with banana and drizzled with honey compote.

LEFTOVER TIP: *Reheat the French toast, covered with a damp paper towel, in the microwave oven the next day in 10-second increments.*

Per Serving Calories: 414; Protein: 17g; Total Carbohydrates: 78g; Sugars: 15g; Fiber: 3g; Total Fat: 6g; Saturated Fat: 2g; Cholesterol: 98mg; Sodium: 716mg

South of the Coast Sweet Potato Toast

30 MINUTES OR LESS, GLUTEN-FREE, VEGETARIAN

SERVES 4

PREP TIME:
5 minutes

COOK TIME:
15 minutes

Crostini is great as a meal, appetizer, or side dish. This recipe puts a twist on a favorite. Using sweet potato as the "crostini" not only makes this a gluten-free alternative to traditional toast, but it is also packed with fiber and vitamin A.

2 plum tomatoes, halved

6 tablespoons extra-virgin olive oil, divided

Salt

Freshly ground black pepper

2 large sweet potatoes, sliced lengthwise

1 cup fresh spinach

8 medium asparagus, trimmed

4 large cooked eggs or egg substitute (poached, scrambled, or fried)

1 cup arugula

4 tablespoons pesto

4 tablespoons shredded Asiago cheese

1. Preheat the oven to 450°F.
2. On a baking sheet, brush the plum tomato halves with 2 tablespoons of olive oil and season with salt and pepper. Roast the tomatoes in the oven for approximately 15 minutes, then remove from the oven and allow to rest.
3. Put the sweet potato slices on a separate baking sheet and brush about 2 tablespoons of oil on each side and season with salt and pepper. Bake the sweet potato slices for about 15 minutes, flipping once after 5 to 7 minutes, until just tender. Remove from the oven and set aside.
4. In a sauté pan or skillet, heat the remaining 2 tablespoons of olive oil over medium heat and sauté the fresh spinach until just wilted. Remove from the pan and rest on a paper-towel-lined dish. In the same pan, add the asparagus and sauté, turning throughout. Transfer to a paper towel-lined dish.

5. Place the slices of grilled sweet potato on serving plates and divide the spinach and asparagus evenly among the slices. Place a prepared egg on top of the spinach and asparagus. Top this with ¼ cup of arugula.

6. Finish by drizzling with 1 tablespoon of pesto and sprinkle with 1 tablespoon of cheese. Serve with 1 roasted plum tomato.

PREP TIP: *Prep the ingredients (except eggs) the day before and make this delicious dish in a flash in the morning. Just reheat the ingredients in the oven, add your eggs, top, and enjoy.*

Per Serving Calories: 441; Protein: 13g; Total Carbohydrates: 23g; Sugars: 9g; Fiber: 4g; Total Fat: 35g; Saturated Fat: 7g; Cholesterol: 217mg; Sodium: 481mg

Zummo Meso Mini Frittatas

GLUTEN-FREE, VEGETARIAN

**SERVES 6
(YIELDS
12 MINI
FRITTATAS)**

PREP TIME:
10 minutes

COOK TIME:
25 minutes

Eggs are such a versatile ingredient, and are used in many dishes, from baked goods and breakfast to binders in some of your favorite dishes and patties to sandwiches and salads. Eggs can be prepared in many ways and enjoyed at any time throughout the day. Quiches are often made with heavy cream and a heavy crust. This cross between a quiche and a muffin is a delicious, gluten-free, nutritious, and filling creation.

Nonstick cooking spray, olive oil, or butter

1½ tablespoons extra-virgin olive oil

¼ cup chopped red potatoes (about 3 small)

¼ cup minced onions

¼ cup chopped red bell pepper

¼ cup asparagus, sliced lengthwise in half and chopped

4 large eggs

4 large egg whites

½ cup skim milk

Salt

Freshly ground black pepper

½ cup shredded low-moisture, part-skim mozzarella cheese, divided

1. Preheat the oven to 350°F. Using nonstick cooking spray, prepare a 12-count muffin pan.
2. In a medium sauté pan or skillet, heat the oil over medium heat and sauté the potatoes and onions for about 4 minutes, until the potatoes are fork-tender.
3. Add the bell pepper and asparagus and sauté for about 4 minutes, until just tender. Transfer the contents of a pan onto a paper-towel-lined plate to cool.
4. In a bowl, whisk together the eggs, egg whites, and milk. Season with salt and pepper.
5. Once the vegetables are cooled to room temperature, add the vegetables and ¼ cup of mozzarella cheese.

6. Using a spoon or ladle, evenly distribute the contents of the bowl into the prepared muffin pan, filling the cups about halfway.
7. Sprinkle the remaining ¼ cup of cheese over the top of the cups.
8. Bake for 20 to 25 minutes, or until eggs reach an internal temperature of 145°F or the center is solid.
9. Allow the mini frittatas to rest for 5 to 10 minutes before removing from muffin pan and serving.

LEFTOVER TIP: *You can wrap and freeze these for up to 2 months.*

VARIATION TIP: *Throw in your favorite ingredients to create a variety of protein-packed snacks. Try adding crumbled bacon or chicken sausage on top for even more flavor and protein.*

Per Serving (2 mini frittatas) Calories: 133; Protein: 10g; Total Carbohydrates: 4g; Sugars: 2g; Fiber: 1g; Total Fat: 9g; Saturated Fat: 3g; Cholesterol: 129mg; Sodium: 151mg

C+C Overnight Oats

DAIRY-FREE, VEGAN

SERVES 2

PREP TIME:
5 minutes, plus 8 hours refrigeration

I'm pretty sure I can make this one in my sleep by now. It's an easy dish that takes only a few minutes to put together.

½ cup vanilla, unsweetened almond milk (not Silk brand)

½ cup rolled oats

2 tablespoons sliced almonds

2 tablespoons simple sugar liquid sweetener

1 teaspoon chia seeds

¼ teaspoon ground cardamom

¼ teaspoon ground cinnamon

In a mason jar, combine the almond milk, oats, almonds, liquid sweetener, chia seeds, cardamom, and cinnamon and shake well. Store in the refrigerator for 8 to 24 hours, then serve cold or heated.

VARIATION TIP: *For a gluten-free version of this dish, use gluten-free instant oats.*

Per Serving Calories: 131; Protein: 5g; Total Carbohydrates: 17g; Sugars: 1g; Fiber: 4g; Total Fat: 6g; Saturated Fat: <1g; Cholesterol: 0mg; Sodium: 45mg

Sunshine Overnight Oats

DAIRY-FREE, VEGETARIAN

SERVES 2

PREP TIME:
5 minutes, plus 8 hours refrigeration

Turmeric is a fun spice. It can change the flavor and color of your dish. I can't help but smile whenever I eat this, because it looks almost fake with its bright-yellow color from the turmeric and red streaks from the raspberries.

⅔ cup vanilla, unsweetened almond milk (not Silk brand)

⅓ cup rolled oats

¼ cup raspberries

1 teaspoon honey

¼ teaspoon turmeric

⅛ teaspoon ground cinnamon

Pinch ground cloves

In a mason jar, combine the almond milk, oats, raspberries, honey, turmeric, cinnamon, and cloves and shake well. Store in the refrigerator for 8 to 24 hours, then serve cold or heated.

VARIATION TIP: *Because overnight oats are made to be left-overs, I throw in fresh berries and chopped nuts for crunch and variety.*

Per Serving Calories: 82; Protein: 2g; Total Carbohydrates: 14g; Sugars: 4g; Fiber: 3g; Total Fat: 2g; Saturated Fat: 0g; Cholesterol: 0mg; Sodium: 98mg

Spinach Pie

VEGETARIAN

SERVES 8

PREP TIME:
10 minutes

COOK TIME:
25 minutes

I remember making this breakfast with my grandmother. She taught me how to assemble it with hand motions and gestures because she spoke little English and my 10-year-old self was still trying to master English as well. I hope your heart is as happy as mine after making this one.

Nonstick cooking spray

2 tablespoons extra-virgin olive oil

1 onion, chopped

1 pound frozen spinach, thawed

¼ teaspoon garlic salt

¼ teaspoon freshly ground black pepper

¼ teaspoon ground nutmeg

4 large eggs, divided

1 cup grated Parmesan cheese, divided

2 puff pastry doughs, (organic, if available), at room temperature

4 hard-boiled eggs, halved

1. Preheat the oven to 350°F. Spray a baking sheet with nonstick cooking spray and set aside.
2. Heat a large sauté pan or skillet over medium-high heat. Put in the oil and onion and cook for about 5 minutes, until translucent.
3. Squeeze the excess water from the spinach, then add to the pan and cook, uncovered, so that any excess water from the spinach can evaporate. Add the garlic salt, pepper, and nutmeg. Remove from heat and set aside to cool.
4. In a small bowl, crack 3 eggs and mix well. Add the eggs and ½ cup Parmesan cheese to the cooled spinach mix.
5. On the prepared baking sheet, roll out the pastry dough. Layer the spinach mix on top of dough, leaving 2 inches around each edge.
6. Once the spinach is spread onto the pastry dough, place hard-boiled egg halves evenly throughout the pie, then cover with the second pastry dough. Pinch the edges closed.

7. Crack the remaining egg in a small bowl and mix well. Brush the egg wash over the pastry dough.
8. Bake for 15 to 20 minutes, until golden brown and warmed through.

SUBSTITUTION TIP: *For a low-carb version of this dish, you can try using thick-cut roasted zucchini as the base, skipping the pastry dough on the bottom.*

LEFTOVER TIP: *Store in a large container; reheat in the microwave for 15 seconds, then 5 minutes in a toaster oven.*

Per Serving Calories: 417; Protein: 17g; Total Carbohydrates: 25g; Sugars: 1g; Fiber: 3g; Total Fat: 28g; Saturated Fat: 7g, Cholesterol: 210mg; Sodium: 490mg

Almond Flour Pancakes with Berry and Honey Compote

30 MINUTES OR LESS, GLUTEN-FREE, VEGETARIAN

SERVES 4

PREP TIME:
5 minutes

COOK TIME:
15 minutes

This was my first and only pancake recipe for years. The fruit is key for fully cooked 'cakes in this recipe. The pancake steams in the water escaping from the cooking fruit.

1 cup almond flour

1 cup plus 2 tablespoons skim milk

2 large eggs, beaten

⅓ cup honey

1 teaspoon baking soda

¼ teaspoon salt

2 tablespoons extra-virgin olive oil

1 sliced banana or 1 cup sliced strawberries, divided

2 tablespoons Berry and Honey Compote (page 189)

1. In a bowl, mix together the almond flour, milk, eggs, honey, baking soda, and salt.
2. In a large sauté pan or skillet, heat the olive oil over medium-high heat and pour ⅓ cup pancake batter into the pan. Cook for 2 to 3 minutes. Right before pancake is ready to flip, add half of the fresh fruit and flip to cook for 2 to 3 minutes on the other side, until cooked through.
3. Top with the remaining fruit, drizzle with Berry and Honey Compote and serve.

Per Serving Calories: 415; Protein: 12g; Total Carbohydrates: 46g; Sugars: 38g; Fiber: 4g; Total Fat: 24g; Saturated Fat: 3g; Cholesterol: 94mg; Sodium: 526mg

Herby Tomato Soup, page 61

Soups and Salads

Lemon Orzo Chicken Soup

**30 MINUTES
OR LESS,
DAIRY-FREE,
ONE POT**

SERVES 8

PREP TIME:
10 minutes

COOK TIME:
20 minutes

I could eat this soup every day of the week. It's hearty but light, flavorful but not overbearing.

**1 tablespoon
extra-virgin olive oil**

1 cup chopped onion

½ cup chopped carrots

½ cup chopped celery

3 garlic cloves, minced

**9 cups low-sodium
chicken broth**

**2 cups shredded cooked
chicken breast**

**½ cup freshly squeezed
lemon juice**

Zest of 1 lemon, grated

**1 to 2 teaspoons
dried oregano**

8 ounces cooked orzo pasta

1. In a large pot, heat the oil over medium heat and add the onion, carrots, celery, and garlic and cook for about 5 minutes, until the onions are translucent. Add the broth and bring to a boil.
2. Reduce to a simmer, cover, and cook for 10 more minutes, until the flavors meld. Then add the shredded chicken, lemon juice and zest, and oregano.
3. Plate the orzo in serving bowls first, then add the chicken soup.

PREP TIP: *Buy rotisserie chicken to save a step. Let cool completely before shredding.*

Per Serving Calories: 215; Protein: 16g; Total Carbohydrates: 27g; Sugars: 2g; Fiber: 2g; Total Fat: 5g; Saturated Fat: 1g; Cholesterol: 26mg; Sodium: 114mg

Spanish Potato Salad

30 MINUTES OR LESS, GLUTEN-FREE, ONE POT VEGETARIAN

SERVES 6 TO 8

PREP TIME:
10 minutes

COOK TIME:
10 minutes

The creamy dressing created here coats the potatoes in a velvety, intoxicating flavor. I definitely portion this dish carefully. If you love the saltiness of Spanish olives, you will love the way they cut through the dense salad.

4 russet potatoes, peeled and chopped

3 large hard-boiled eggs, chopped

1 cup frozen mixed vegetables, thawed

½ cup plain, unsweetened, full-fat Greek yogurt

5 tablespoons pitted Spanish olives

½ teaspoon freshly ground black pepper

½ teaspoon dried mustard seed

½ tablespoon freshly squeezed lemon juice

½ teaspoon dried dill

Salt

Freshly ground black pepper

1. Boil potatoes for 5 to 7 minutes, until just fork-tender, checking periodically for doneness. You don't want to overcook them.
2. While the potatoes are cooking, in a large bowl, mix the eggs, vegetables, yogurt, olives, pepper, mustard, lemon juice, and dill. Season with salt and pepper. Once the potatoes are cooled somewhat, add them to the large bowl, then mix well and serve.

LEFTOVER TIP: *This dish tastes even better the next day, after the flavors have time to set overnight. It makes for a great meal prepping recipe.*

Per Serving Calories: 192; Protein: 9g; Total Carbohydrates: 30g; Sugars: 3g; Fiber: 2g; Total Fat: 5g; Saturated Fat: 1g; Cholesterol: 96mg; Sodium: 59mg

Curry Zucchini Soup

**30 MINUTES
OR LESS,
DAIRY-FREE,
GLUTEN-FREE,
ONE POT**

**SERVES
4 TO 6**

PREP TIME:
10 minutes

COOK TIME:
20 minutes

This brothy soup gets a nice punch of flavor from the addition of curry powder. You can adjust the amount of curry based on your preference to make this soup your own.

¼ **cup extra-virgin olive oil**

**1 medium onion,
chopped (about ½ cup)**

1 carrot, shredded

1 small garlic clove, minced

**4 cups low-sodium
chicken broth**

**2 medium zucchini,
thinly sliced**

**2 apples, peeled
and chopped**

**2½ teaspoons
curry powder**

¼ **teaspoon salt**

1. In a large pot, heat the oil over medium heat. Sauté the onion, carrot, and garlic and cook until tender. Add the chicken broth, zucchini, apples, and curry powder.
2. Boil for 2 minutes, reduce the heat, and simmer for 20 minutes, until the vegetables are tender.
3. Season with the salt and serve.

INGREDIENT TIP: *You can prep the carrots, garlic, onion, and zucchini up to 3 days in advance to reduce prep time on the day of cooking.*

LEFTOVER TIP: *You can freeze this soup for up to 6 months.*

Per Serving Calories: 208; Protein: 4g; Total Carbohydrates: 19g; Sugars: 11g; Fiber: 4g; Total Fat: 14g; Saturated Fat: 2g; Cholesterol: 0mg; Sodium: 237mg

Rustic Winter Salad

30 MINUTES OR LESS, GLUTEN-FREE, ONE POT VEGETARIAN

SERVES 4

PREP TIME:
10 minutes

After a long work trip or a week of eating out, I crave this salad. The light but noteworthy salad dressing keeps you coming back bite after bite.

1 small green apple, thinly sliced

6 stalks kale, stems removed and greens roughly chopped

½ cup crumbled feta cheese

½ cup dried currants

½ cup chopped pitted kalamata olives

½ cup thinly sliced radicchio

2 scallions, both green and white parts, thinly sliced

¼ cup peeled, julienned carrots

2 celery stalks, thinly sliced

¼ cup Sweet Red Wine Vinaigrette (page 185)

Salt (optional)

Freshly ground black pepper (optional)

In a large bowl, combine the apple, kale, feta, currants, olives, radicchio, scallions, carrots, and celery and mix well. Drizzle with the vinaigrette. Season with salt and pepper (if using), then serve.

LEFTOVER TIP: *Store salad and dressing separately.*

VARIATION TIP: *Add some grilled chicken and you have a great work lunch. Store the dressing on the side and toss right before eating.*

Per Serving Calories: 253; Protein: 6g; Total Carbohydrates: 29g; Sugars: 19g; Fiber: 4g; Total Fat: 15g; Saturated Fat: 4g; Cholesterol: 17mg; Sodium: 480mg

Yellow and White Hearts of Palm Salad

30 MINUTES OR LESS, DAIRY-FREE, VEGETARIAN

SERVES 4

PREP TIME:
10 minutes

I can hear my childhood self giggling in my grandmother's 1980s kitchen when I make this salad. Since this is a relatively safe-to-make dish, after the veggies were chopped, I was allowed to put everything together and "help" my grandma.

2 (14-ounce) cans hearts of palm, drained and cut into ½-inch-thick slices

1 avocado, cut into ½-inch pieces

1 cup halved yellow cherry tomatoes

½ small shallot, thinly sliced

¼ cup coarsely chopped flat-leaf parsley

2 tablespoons low-fat mayonnaise

2 tablespoons extra-virgin olive oil

¼ teaspoon salt

⅛ teaspoon freshly ground black pepper

1. In a large bowl, toss the hearts of palm, avocado, tomatoes, shallot, and parsley.
2. In a small bowl, whisk the mayonnaise, olive oil, salt, and pepper, then mix into the large bowl.

INGREDIENT TIP: *Add fresh-squeezed lemon juice to brighten up the dish before eating.*

Per Serving Calories: 192; Protein: 5g; Total Carbohydrates: 14g; Sugars: 2g; Fiber: 7g; Total Fat: 15g; Saturated Fat: 2g; Cholesterol: 0mg; Sodium: 841mg

Herby Tomato Soup

SERVES 2

PREP TIME:
10 minutes

COOK TIME:
10 minutes

Warm tomato soup can cure most ailments. There is a great yin and yang happening here between the sweet from the basil and the tart from the tomatoes. Go on, try it for yourself.

¼ cup extra-virgin olive oil

2 garlic cloves, minced

1 (14.5-ounce) can plum tomatoes, whole or diced

1 cup vegetable broth

¼ cup chopped fresh basil

1. In a medium pot, heat the oil over medium heat, then add the garlic and cook for 2 minutes, until fragrant.
2. Meanwhile, in a bowl using an immersion blender or in a blender, puree the tomatoes and their juices.
3. Add the pureed tomatoes and broth to the pot and mix well. Simmer for 10 to 15 minutes and serve, garnished with basil.

INGREDIENT TIP: *If you don't have fresh basil, you can sprinkle dried basil into the soup before serving.*

Per Serving Calories: 307; Protein: 3g; Total Carbohydrates: 11g; Sugars: 10g; Fiber: 4g; Total Fat: 27g; Saturated Fat: 4g; Cholesterol: 0mg; Sodium: 661mg

No-Mayo Florence Tuna Salad

30 MINUTES OR LESS, GLUTEN-FREE, ONE POT

SERVES 4

PREP TIME:
10 minutes

Tuna salad just got an upgrade. Fresh arugula and lemon brighten up this once-typical tuna salad while the cannellini beans round out the savory protein flavors.

4 cups spring mix greens

1 (15-ounce) can cannellini beans, drained

2 (5-ounce) cans water-packed, white albacore tuna, drained (I prefer Wild Planet brand)

⅔ cup crumbled feta cheese

½ cup thinly sliced sun-dried tomatoes

¼ cup sliced pitted kalamata olives

¼ cup thinly sliced scallions, both green and white parts

3 tablespoons extra-virgin olive oil

½ teaspoon dried cilantro

2 or 3 leaves thinly chopped fresh sweet basil

1 lime, zested and juiced

Kosher salt

Freshly ground black pepper

In a large bowl, combine greens, beans, tuna, feta, tomatoes, olives, scallions, olive oil, cilantro, basil, and lime juice and zest. Season with salt and pepper, mix, and enjoy!

VARIATION TIP: *What I love about this dish is that the swap-ins are endless. Is the family getting bored with cannellini beans? Try replacing 50 percent of the beans with lentils or chick-peas. Baby kale or spinach instead of arugula is a great way to introduce different phytonutrients into your diet while adding some variety to this lunch at the same time.*

Per Serving (1 cup) Calories: 355; Protein: 22g; Total Carbohydrates: 25g; Sugars: 5g; Fiber: 8g; Total Fat: 19g; Saturated Fat: 5g; Cholesterol: 47mg; Sodium: 744mg

Artichoke and Broccoli Toss

GLUTEN-FREE, VEGETARIAN

SERVES 2

PREP TIME:
10 minutes, plus 2 hours refrigeration

Ever have one of those days when you open up your pantry and refrigerator and throw together a dish you end up making over and over again? This is one of those dishes. I keep jars of olive oil-marinated artichoke hearts and sun-dried tomatoes on hand for this dish.

2½ cups broccoli slaw

½ cup chopped artichoke hearts

⅓ cup chopped red onion

⅓ cup chopped sun-dried tomatoes

⅓ cup halved pitted kalamata olives

⅓ cup Creamy Citrus Dressing (page 195)

1 small beet, roasted and chopped, for garnish

¼ cup crumbled feta, for garnish

1. In a large bowl, using tongs or—my favorite kitchen tool—your hands, mix together the broccoli slaw, artichoke hearts, onion, sun-dried tomatoes, and olives.
2. Pour the dressing over the broccoli and stir to coat well. Top with the beet and feta.
3. Pop the salad into the refrigerator, covered, for 2 to 8 hours to chill. This will allow the flavors to marry and further develop for a truly delicious dish.

INGREDIENT TIP: *I usually massage the dressing into the broccoli by hand. This helps coat the vegetables more thoroughly.*

Per Serving Calories: 265; Protein: 12g; Total Carbohydrates: 27g; Sugars: 13g; Fiber: 7g; Total Fat: 13g; Saturated Fat: 4g; Cholesterol: 22mg; Sodium: 1,441mg

Mushroom and Potato Stew

GLUTEN-FREE, ONE POT, VEGETARIAN

SERVES 6

PREP TIME:
10 minutes

COOK TIME:
40 minutes

This is hands down my favorite soup to meal prep. I usually double the recipe and store the leftover soup in mason jars. This soup defrosts and reheats just as well as the first day you make it.

2 tablespoons extra-virgin olive oil

5 ounces mushrooms, sliced

½ cup diced carrots

½ cup diced yellow onion

½ cup diced celery

2½ cups low-sodium vegetable broth

1 cup diced tomatoes

1 teaspoon garlic powder

1 bay leaf

1 russet potato, peeled and finely diced

1 cup cooked chickpeas

½ cup crumbled feta, for serving

1. In a large sauté pan or skillet, heat the oil over medium heat. Add the mushrooms and cook for 5 minutes, until they reduce in size and soften.
2. Add the carrots, onion, and celery to the pan and cook for 10 minutes, or until the onions are golden. Pour in the vegetable broth, tomatoes, garlic powder, and bay leaf and bring to a simmer. Add the potato.
3. Mix well and cover. Cook for 20 minutes or until the potato is fork-tender.
4. Add in the chickpeas, stir, and the remove the bay leaf. Season with salt and pepper. Serve, topped with feta, and enjoy!

INGREDIENT TIP: *Be sure to taste the soup as you're seasoning it so that you don't over- or under-season. You can also experiment and add your favorite spices to make this dish your own.*

Per Serving Calories: 162; Protein: 6g; Total Carbohydrates: 19g; Sugars: 4g; Fiber: 4g; Total Fat: 8g; Saturated Fat: 3g; Cholesterol: 11mg; Sodium: 218mg

White Bean and Kale Soup

DAIRY-FREE, GLUTEN-FREE, ONE POT, VEGAN

SERVES 4

PREP TIME: 25 minutes

COOK TIME: 30 minutes

Whenever I make this soup, I think of my restaurant days. I worked at a little Italian restaurant in high school (and part of college), and Tuesday was soup day. The whole restaurant would fill up with the warm smell of chicken broth and simmering vegetables.

1 to 2 tablespoons extra-virgin olive oil

1 large shallot, minced

1 large purple carrot, chopped

1 celery stalk, chopped

1 teaspoon garlic powder

3 cups low-sodium vegetable broth

1 (15-ounce) can cannellini beans

1 cup chopped baby kale

1 teaspoon salt (optional)

½ teaspoon freshly ground black pepper (optional)

1 lemon, juiced and zested

1½ tablespoons chopped fresh thyme (optional)

3 tablespoons chopped fresh oregano (optional)

1. In a large, deep pot, heat the oil. Add the shallot, carrot, celery, and garlic powder and sauté on medium-low heat for 3 to 5 minutes, until the vegetables are golden.
2. Add the vegetable broth and beans and bring to a simmer. Cook for 15 minutes.
3. Add in the kale, salt (if using), and pepper (if using). Cook for another 5 to 10 minutes, until the kale is soft. Right before serving, stir in the lemon juice and zest, thyme (if using), and oregano (if using).

LEFTOVER TIP: *Store in old tomato sauce jars; this makes for easy reheating in the microwave. You can keep these jars in the freezer for up to 6 months.*

Per Serving Calories: 165; Protein: 7g; Total Carbohydrates: 26g; Sugars: 5g; Fiber: 7g; Total Fat: 4g; Saturated Fat: 1g; Cholesterol: 0mg; Sodium: 135mg

Spring Mix with Fig and Citrus Dressing

30 MINUTES OR LESS, GLUTEN-FREE

SERVES 2

PREP TIME:
10 minutes

My mom has always been, and will always remain, the Salad Queen in our family. We have distant relatives still begging for her homemade salad dressings. Here's the thing: She will never write down her recipes, so unless you're blessed enough to eat at her table, you miss out! I like to think this salad is an homage to all her skills.

¼ cup **Skinny Cider Dressing (page 186)**

4 cups **spring mix greens**

⅓ cup **crumbled goat cheese**

3 tablespoons **fig jam**

2 to 3 **heirloom tomatoes, cut into 3-inch chunks**

1 to 2 tablespoons **balsamic glaze**

6 slices **prosciutto, rolled**

1. In a large bowl, drizzle the dressing over the salad greens, and toss well.
2. In a separate bowl, whisk the goat cheese and jam together and set aside.
3. Put the salad mix in serving bowls, top with the tomatoes, then drizzle the cheese mixture over dish.
4. Finish the dish with a drizzle of balsamic glaze and top with the prosciutto.

INGREDIENT TIP: *If you regularly refrigerate your balsamic glaze, make sure it returns to room temperature before using it in a salad.*

Per Serving Calories: 375; Protein: 23g; Total Carbohydrates: 30g; Sugars: 24g; Fiber: 3g; Total Fat: 15g; Saturated Fat: 7g; Cholesterol: 77mg; Sodium: 2,160mg

Tricolor Tomato Summer Salad

30 MINUTES OR LESS, GLUTEN-FREE, VEGETARIAN

SERVES 3 TO 4

PREP TIME:
10 minutes

This salad was always present at summer barbecues at the shore. The sweet tomatoes and vinegar are almost enough to make you pucker when you take your first bite.

¼ cup while balsamic vinegar

2 tablespoons Dijon mustard

1 tablespoon sugar

½ teaspoon freshly ground black pepper

½ teaspoon garlic salt

¼ cup extra-virgin olive oil

1½ cups chopped orange, yellow, and red tomatoes

½ cucumber, peeled and diced

1 small red onion, thinly sliced

¼ cup crumbled feta (optional)

1. In a small bowl, whisk the vinegar, mustard, sugar, pepper, and garlic salt. Next, slowly whisk in the olive oil.
2. In a large bowl, add the tomatoes, cucumber, and red onion. Add the dressing. Toss once or twice, and serve with feta crumbles (if using) on top.

PREP TIP: *If you want to prep this recipe ahead of time, store the dressing separately from the salad until you are ready to serve it.*

Per Serving Calories: 246; Protein: 1g; Total Carbohydrates: 19g; Sugars: 13g; Fiber: 2g; Total Fat: 18g; Saturated Fat: 3g; Cholesterol: 0mg; Sodium: 483mg

Vegetarian Chili

**DAIRY-FREE,
GLUTEN-FREE,
VEGETARIAN**

> SERVES
> 6 TO 8

PREP TIME:
15 minutes

COOK TIME:
45 minutes

What I love about this dish is that you can get almost everything for it in your pantry. No crazy ingredients, just delicious cooking. Before enjoying, I add a dollop of full-fat sour cream and a squeeze of lemon.

**2 tablespoons
extra-virgin olive oil**

**2 carrots, peeled
and chopped**

**½ large yellow
onion, chopped**

5 garlic cloves, minced

**1 large zucchini,
finely chopped**

**4 cups low-sodium
vegetable broth**

**1 (14.5-ounce) can
diced tomatoes**

¼ cup tomato paste

2½ teaspoons chili powder

1 teaspoon sweet paprika

1 teaspoon ground cumin

½ teaspoon ground allspice

Salt

**Freshly ground
black pepper**

½ cup water

**4 tablespoons gluten-free
all-purpose flour**

**2 (15-ounce) cans
chickpeas, drained
and rinsed**

**2 (15-ounce) cans kidney
beans, drained and rinsed**

**1 cup plain, unsweetened,
full-fat Greek yogurt,
for serving**

1. In a large pot, heat the olive oil over medium heat. Add the carrots, onion, and garlic and cook for about 4 minutes, tossing regularly, until softened. Add the zucchini and cook for about 4 minutes, until softened.

2. Add the broth, tomatoes and their juices, tomato paste, chili powder, paprika, cumin, and allspice. Season with salt and pepper. Bring to a boil.

3. Meanwhile, in a small bowl, pour in the water and the flour, stirring the flour in 1 tablespoon at a time, until mixed.

4. Mix chickpeas and kidney beans into the pot of chili and stir until completely combined. To thicken the chili, add the flour mixture 1 tablespoon at a time, stirring well with each addition. Lower the heat and simmer for 25 minutes, until thickened.

5. Serve with a dollop of full-fat, plain Greek yogurt.

VARIATION TIP: *Use half the amount of beans in this recipe and use 1 pound lean ground turkey to change up this recipe. You can also experiment with toppings, such as diced avocado.*

LEFTOVER TIP: *Store chili in old tomato sauce jars. They reheat twice as fast in the microwave oven for a quick and home-made lunch. You can also freeze them for up to 6 months.*

Per Serving Calories: 430; Protein: 22g; Total Carbohydrates: 67g; Sugars: 10g; Fiber: 17g; Total Fat: 8g; Saturated Fat: 2g; Cholesterol: 5mg; Sodium: 354mg

Mediterranean Bruschetta Hummus Platter, page 75

Snacks and Sides

Walnut and Freekeh Pilaf

30 MINUTES OR LESS

SERVES 4

PREP TIME:
15 minutes

COOK TIME:
15 minutes

Freekeh, a hearty whole grain, is great to use in salads like this because it keeps its integrity throughout the cooking process. The cinnamon, allspice, and lemon juice create an awesome flavor combination.

2½ cups freekeh

3 tablespoons extra-virgin olive oil, divided

2 medium onions, diced

¼ teaspoon ground cinnamon

¼ teaspoon ground allspice

5 cups chicken stock

½ cup chopped walnuts

Salt

Freshly ground black pepper

½ cup plain, unsweetened, full-fat Greek yogurt

1½ teaspoons freshly squeezed lemon juice

½ teaspoon garlic powder

1. In a small bowl, soak the freekeh covered in cold water for 5 minutes. Drain and rinse the freekeh, then rinse one more time.
2. In a large sauté pan or skillet, heat 2 tablespoons oil, then add the onions and cook until fragrant. Add the freekeh, cinnamon, and allspice. Stir periodically for 1 minute.
3. Add the stock and walnuts and season with salt and pepper. Bring to a simmer.
4. Cover and reduce the heat to low. Cook for 15 minutes. Once freekeh is tender, remove from the heat and allow to rest for 5 minutes.
5. In a small bowl, combine the yogurt, lemon juice, and garlic powder. You may need to add salt to bring out the flavors. Add the yogurt mixture to the freekeh and serve immediately.

VARIATION TIP: *You can add dried fruit to this for a sweet crunch. I usually add cranberries for a different twist.*

Per Serving Calories: 653; Protein: 23g; Total Carbohydrates: 91g; Sugars: 4g; Fiber: 12g; Total Fat: 25g; Saturated Fat: 3g; Cholesterol: 4mg; Sodium: 575mg

Easy Italian Roasted Vegetables

DAIRY-FREE, GLUTEN-FREE, VEGAN

SERVES 6

PREP TIME:
15 minutes

COOK TIME:
45 minutes

I usually have crusty bread handy when I dig into this vegetable side. The natural sauce this dish makes is incredible. Once you make this dish twice, you'll be throwing it together during your next family dinner.

Nonstick cooking spray

2 eggplants, peeled and sliced ⅛ inch thick

1 zucchini, sliced ¼ inch thick

1 yellow summer squash, sliced ¼ inch thick

2 Roma tomatoes, sliced ⅛ inch thick

¼ cup, plus 2 tablespoons extra-virgin olive oil, divided

1 tablespoon garlic powder

¼ teaspoon dried oregano

¼ teaspoon dried basil

¼ teaspoon salt

Freshly ground black pepper

1. Preheat the oven to 400°F.
2. Spray a 9-by-13-inch baking dish with cooking spray. In the dish, toss the eggplant, zucchini, squash, and tomatoes with 2 tablespoons oil, garlic powder, oregano, basil, salt, and pepper.
3. Standing the vegetables up (like little soldiers), alternate layers of eggplant, zucchini, squash, and Roma tomato.
4. Drizzle the top with the remaining ¼ cup of olive oil.
5. Bake, uncovered, for 40 to 45 minutes, or until vegetables are golden brown.

VARIATION TIP: *For a sweet note, consider adding sautéed shallots and/or roasted red bell peppers.*

Per Serving Calories: 186; Protein: 3g; Total Carbohydrates: 15g; Sugars: 9g; Fiber: 5g; Total Fat: 14g; Saturated Fat: 2g; Cholesterol: 0mg; Sodium: 110mg

Mediterranean Crostini

30 MINUTES OR LESS, VEGETARIAN

SERVES 6

PREP TIME:
15 minutes

COOK TIME:
10 minutes

The textures of this dish made me fall in love with it. The crunch of the toast and velvety hummus keep everything together. Topping each slice with fresh cucumbers, olives, and feta makes for a fun and delicious appetizer or side.

1 baguette, sliced ¼ inch thick

5 tablespoons extra-virgin olive oil

¼ teaspoon salt

⅛ teaspoon freshly ground black pepper

½ cup store-bought hummus or Garlic-Lemon Hummus (page 76)

1 cup quartered grape tomatoes

1 cup diced cucumber

4 chopped pitted kalamata olives

½ cup crumbled feta cheese

½ cup chopped flat-leaf parsley, for garnish

⅓ cup Pickled Turnips (page 187) (optional)

1. Preheat the oven to 350°F.
2. On baking sheets, arrange the baguette slices and carefully brush the tops and sides with the oil. Sprinkle with salt and pepper.
3. Bake for 10 minutes or until the toasts become slightly crispy. Remove them from the oven and set aside.
4. Once the slices are cool enough to handle, spread a thin layer of hummus on the toast.
5. Individually, spoon tomatoes, cucumber, olives, and feta cheese onto the toast. Garnish with fresh parsley and pickled turnips.

PREP TIP: *Slice and dice the cucumber, olive, feta, and grape tomatoes up to 1 day prior to save time.*

Per Serving Calories: 436; Protein: 14g; Total Carbohydrates: 55g; Sugars: 2g; Fiber: 3g; Total Fat: 19g; Saturated Fat: 4g; Cholesterol: 11mg; Sodium: 1,042mg

Mediterranean Bruschetta Hummus Platter

30 MINUTES OR LESS, VEGETARIAN

SERVES 6

PREP TIME:
15 minutes

If you find someone who can't find something on this platter to eat, call me! The balsamic glaze cuts sharply through the hummus and brightens the dip, while the fresh, sweet tomato and herbed oil bring me back to summers at the beach.

½ cup finely diced
fresh tomato

⅓ cup finely diced seedless
English cucumber

1 teaspoon extra-virgin
olive oil

1 (10-ounce) container
plain hummus

2 tablespoons
balsamic glaze

2 tablespoons crumbled
feta cheese

1 tablespoon fresh
chopped parsley or basil

¼ cup Herbed Oil
(page 184)

4 warmed pitas, cut into
wedges, for serving

Carrot sticks, for serving

Celery sticks, for serving

Sliced bell peppers,
for serving

Broccoli, for serving

Purple cauliflower,
for serving

1. In a small bowl, mix the tomato and cucumber and toss with the olive oil. Pile the cucumber mixture over a fresh container of hummus. Drizzle the hummus and vegetables with the balsamic glaze. Top with crumbled feta and fresh parsley.
2. Put the hummus on a large cutting board. Pour the Herbed Oil in a small bowl and put it on the cutting board. Surround the bowls with the pita wedges and cut carrot sticks, celery sticks, sliced bell peppers, broccoli, and cauliflower.

VARIATION TIP: *This plate can be easily adjusted for dairy-free or gluten-free diets by forgoing the feta cheese and pita.*

Per Serving Calories: 345; Protein: 9g; Total Carbohydrates: 32g; Sugars: 3g; Fiber: 3g; Total Fat: 19g; Saturated Fat: 4g; Cholesterol: 3mg; Sodium: 473mg

Garlic-Lemon Hummus

30 MINUTES OR LESS, DAIRY-FREE, GLUTEN-FREE, VEGAN

SERVES 6

PREP TIME:
15 minutes

The scent of lemon released while blending this hummus is refreshing and relaxing. I can't help but find myself slowing my pace and breathing easier whenever I'm in the kitchen making this lemony dip.

1 (15-ounce) can chickpeas, drained and rinsed

4 to 5 tablespoons tahini (sesame seed paste)

4 tablespoons extra-virgin olive oil, divided

2 lemons, juice

1 lemon, zested, divided

1 tablespoon minced garlic

Pinch salt

1. In a food processor, combine the chickpeas, tahini, 2 tablespoons of olive oil, lemon juice, half of the lemon zest, and garlic and blend for up to 1 minute. After 30 seconds of blending, stop and scrape the sides down with a spatula, before blending for another 30 seconds. At this point, you've made hummus! Taste and add salt as desired. Feel free to add 1 teaspoon of water at a time to help thin the hummus to a better consistency.

2. Scoop the hummus into a bowl, then drizzle with the remaining 2 tablespoons of olive oil and remaining lemon zest.

LEFTOVER TIP: *This will last in the refrigerator in an airtight container for up to 7 days. It works great as spread on sandwiches and wraps for extra flavor and protein.*

Per Serving Calories: 216; Protein: 5g; Total Carbohydrates: 17g; Sugars: <1g; Fiber: 5g; Total Fat: 15g; Saturated Fat: 2g; Cholesterol: 0mg; Sodium: 12mg

Mediterranean Trail Mix

30 MINUTES OR LESS, DAIRY-FREE, GLUTEN-FREE, VEGAN

SERVES 6

PREP TIME:
5 minutes

The natural sugars from dates, apricots, and figs play off the salty and savory walnuts, almonds, and pistachios. This is a colorful, healthy, minimally processed snack that I hope you enjoy.

1 cup roughly chopped unsalted walnuts

½ cup roughly chopped salted almonds

½ cup shelled salted pistachios

½ cup roughly chopped apricots

½ cup roughly chopped dates

⅓ cup dried figs, sliced in half

In a large zip-top bag, combine the walnuts, almonds, pistachios, apricots, dates, and figs and mix well.

VARIATION TIP: *Add in 1 to 2 cups plain popcorn per serving to make this snack even heartier.*

Per Serving Calories: 348; Protein: 9g; Total Carbohydrates: 33g; Sugars: 22g; Fiber: 7g; Total Fat: 24g; Saturated Fat: 2g; Cholesterol: 0mg; Sodium: 95mg

Savory Mediterranean Popcorn

30 MINUTES OR LESS, DAIRY-FREE, GLUTEN-FREE, VEGAN

SERVES 4 TO 6

PREP TIME:
5 minutes

COOK TIME:
2 minutes

Your next movie night needs this popcorn. The thyme and oregano balance the stronger flavors of the garlic powder and freshly ground black pepper in this popcorn snack. This popcorn is a good source of fiber.

3 tablespoons extra-virgin olive oil

¼ teaspoon garlic powder

¼ teaspoon freshly ground black pepper

¼ teaspoon sea salt

⅛ teaspoon dried thyme

⅛ teaspoon dried oregano

12 cups plain popped popcorn

1. In a large sauté pan or skillet, heat the oil over medium heat, until shimmering, and then add the garlic powder, pepper, salt, thyme, and oregano until fragrant.
2. In a large bowl, drizzle the oil over the popcorn, toss, and serve.

VARIATION TIP: *Make this dish fun with color by adding ⅛ teaspoon paprika to the blend for a red-tinted snack.*

Per Serving Calories: 183; Protein: 3g; Total Carbohydrates: 19g; Sugars: 0g; Fiber: 4g; Total Fat: 12g; Saturated Fat: 2g; Cholesterol: 0mg; Sodium: 146mg

Turkish-Spiced Nuts

**30 MINUTES
OR LESS,
DAIRY-FREE,
GLUTEN-FREE,
VEGAN**

SERVES
4 TO 6

PREP TIME:
10 minutes

COOK TIME:
5 minutes

These strongly flavored nuts are great as an addition to a cheese board, a salad, in trail mix, or on their own. I try to limit the serving of nuts and seeds to ¼ cup at a time.

**1 tablespoon
extra-virgin olive oil**

**1 cup mixed nuts (walnuts,
almonds, cashews, peanuts)**

2 tablespoons paprika

1 tablespoon dried mint

**½ tablespoon
ground cinnamon**

½ tablespoon kosher salt

¼ tablespoon garlic powder

**¼ teaspoon freshly
ground black pepper**

**⅛ tablespoon
ground cumin**

1. In a small to medium saucepan, heat the oil on low heat.
2. Once the oil is warm, add the nuts, paprika, mint, cinnamon, salt, garlic powder, pepper, and cumin and stir continually until the spices are well incorporated with the nuts.

PREP TIP: *Blend the above spices ahead of time to cut your prep time in half.*

Per Serving Calories: 204; Protein: 6g; Total Carbohydrates: 10g; Sugars: 2g; Fiber: 4g; Total Fat: 18g; Saturated Fat: 2g; Cholesterol: 0mg; Sodium: 874mg

Lemony Orzo

30 MINUTES OR LESS, ONE POT, VEGETARIAN

YIELD
2 CUPS

PREP TIME:
5 minutes

COOK TIME:
5 minutes

Orzo is a lighter alternative to pasta—and often less processed—but slightly more filling than rice. The grape tomatoes, orzo, and feta play a great balancing act in flavors.

1 cup dry orzo

1 cup halved grape tomatoes

1 (6-ounce) bag baby spinach

2 tablespoons extra-virgin olive oil

¼ teaspoon salt

Freshly ground black pepper

¾ cup crumbled feta cheese

1 lemon, juiced and zested

1. Bring a medium pot of water to a boil. Stir in the orzo and cook uncovered for 8 minutes. Drain the water, then return the orzo to medium heat.
2. Add in the tomatoes and spinach and cook until the spinach is wilted. Add the oil, salt, and pepper and mix well. Top the dish with feta, lemon juice, and lemon zest, then toss one or two more times and enjoy!

VARIATION TIP: *For additional fiber and protein, try whole-wheat orzo. You can even find gluten-free orzo for a gluten-free version of this dish.*

Per Serving (1 cup) Calories: 610; Protein: 21g; Total Carbohydrates: 74g; Sugars: 6g; Fiber: 6g; Total Fat: 27g; Saturated Fat: 10g; Cholesterol: 50mg; Sodium: 990mg

Puff Pastry Turnover with Roasted Vegetables

VEGETARIAN

SERVES
4 TO 6

PREP TIME:
10 minutes

COOK TIME:
35 minutes

Do you have a loved one who won't eat vegetables? If you wrap veggies in pastry dough, people tend to linger longer over the vegetable platter. The roasted zucchini soaks up so much flavor that it melts in your mouth like butter. These turnovers cook quickly; I usually check on them every 2 to 3 minutes, after they've cooked for 5 minutes.

Nonstick cooking spray

1 zucchini, cut in ¼-inch-thick slices

½ bunch asparagus, cut into quarters

1 package (6-inch) whole-grain pastry discs, in the freezer section (Goya brand preferred), at room temperature

1 large egg, beaten

1. Preheat the oven to 350°F.
2. Spray a baking sheet with cooking spray and arrange the zucchini and asparagus on it in a single layer. Roast for 15 to 20 minutes, until tender. Set aside to cool.
3. Allow the pastry dough to warm to room temperature. Place the discs on a floured surface.
4. Place a roasted zucchini slice on one half of each disc, then top with asparagus. Fold the empty side over the full side and pinch the turnover closed with a fork.
5. Once all discs are full and closed, brush the turnovers with the beaten egg and put them onto a baking sheet. Bake for 10 to 15 minutes, until golden brown. Let cool completely before eating.

SUBSTITUTION TIP: *If zucchini and asparagus aren't to your liking, try using roasted peppers and onions. You can really customize these to suit anyone's palate.*

Per Serving Calories: 334; Protein: 9g; Total Carbohydrates: 42g; Sugars: 3g; Fiber: 4g; Total Fat: 15g; Saturated Fat: 8g; Cholesterol:47mg; Sodium: 741mg

Turmeric-Spiced Crunchy Chickpeas

DAIRY-FREE, GLUTEN-FREE, VEGAN

SERVES 4

PREP TIME:
15 minutes

COOK TIME:
30 minutes

This simply spiced dish is a great snack on its own, or it can be enjoyed atop a salad. Chickpeas offer a one-two punch with their perfectly balanced protein-fiber content, making them a source of sustainable and focused energy.

2 (15-ounce) cans organic chickpeas, drained and rinsed

3 tablespoons extra-virgin olive oil

2 teaspoons Turkish or smoked paprika

2 teaspoons turmeric

½ teaspoon dried oregano

½ teaspoon salt

¼ teaspoon ground ginger

⅛ teaspoon ground white pepper (optional)

1. Preheat the oven to 400°F. Line a baking sheet with parchment paper and set aside.
2. Completely dry the chickpeas. Lay the chickpeas out on a baking sheet, roll them around with paper towels, and allow them to air-dry. I usually let them dry for at least 2½ hours, but can also be left to dry overnight.
3. In a medium bowl, combine the olive oil, paprika, turmeric, oregano, salt, ginger, and white pepper (if using).
4. Add the dry chickpeas to the bowl and toss to combine.
5. Put the chickpeas on the prepared baking sheet and cook for 30 minutes, or until the chickpeas turn golden brown. At 15 minutes, move the chickpeas around on the baking sheet to avoid burning. Check every 10 minutes in case the chickpeas begin to crisp up before the full cooking time has elapsed.
6. Remove from the oven and set them aside to cool.

INGREDIENT TIP: *My recipe uses canned chickpeas. A less-processed approach would be to cook beans from their dried state. You can soak 8 ounces of dried chickpeas overnight, with cold water covering the beans by 3 inches; be sure to add a tablespoon of kosher salt and, if you'd like, add some dried herbs (like oregano or bay leaf). When you're ready to cook, drain the chickpeas and simmer them in salted water for about an hour or until desired tenderness is achieved.*

Per Serving (½ cup) Calories: 308; Protein: 11g; Total Carbohydrates: 40g; Sugars: <1g; Fiber: 11g; Total Fat: 13g; Saturated Fat: 2g; Cholesterol: 0mg; Sodium: 292mg

Crispy Garlic Oven Potatoes

DAIRY-FREE, GLUTEN-FREE, VEGAN

SERVES 2

PREP TIME:
30 minutes

COOK TIME:
30 minutes

Welcome to my version of steak fries! These oven-roasted potatoes are mouthwateringly savory and salty. The dried garlic and onion salt come through well in the crust of these potatoes.

10 ounces golden mini potatoes, halved

4 tablespoons extra-virgin olive oil

2 teaspoons dried, minced garlic

1 teaspoon onion salt

½ teaspoon paprika

¼ teaspoon freshly ground black pepper

¼ teaspoon red pepper flakes

¼ teaspoon dried dill

1. Preheat the oven to 400°F.
2. Soak the potatoes and put in a bowl of ice water for 30 minutes. Change the water if you return and the water is milky.
3. Rinse and dry the potatoes, then put them on a baking sheet.
4. Drizzle the potatoes with oil and sprinkle with the garlic, onion salt, paprika, pepper, red pepper flakes, and dill. Using tongs or your hands, toss well to coat.
5. Lower the heat to 375°F, add potatoes to the oven, and bake for 20 minutes.
6. At 20 minutes, check and flip potatoes. Bake for another 10 minutes, or until the potatoes are fork-tender.

SUBSTITUTION TIP: *Swap sweet potatoes for the golden mini potatoes for a sweeter twist on this savory dish.*

Per Serving (½ cup servings) Calories: 344; Protein: 3g; Total Carbohydrates: 24g; Sugars: 1g; Fiber: 4g; Total Fat: 28g; Saturated Fat: 4g; Cholesterol: 0mg; Sodium: 723mg

Lentil Burgers, page 104

CHAPTER 7

Vegetarian Mains

Rustic Vegetable and Brown Rice Bowl

30 MINUTES OR LESS, DAIRY-FREE, GLUTEN-FREE, VEGETARIAN

SERVES 4

PREP TIME:
15 minutes

COOK TIME:
20 minutes

Don't let preconceived notions about brown rice get in your way of enjoying this dish. This versatile grain is packed with protein, fiber, and B vitamins.

Nonstick cooking spray

2 cups broccoli florets

2 cups cauliflower florets

1 (15-ounce) can chickpeas, drained and rinsed

1 cup carrots sliced 1 inch thick

2 to 3 tablespoons extra-virgin olive oil, divided

Salt

Freshly ground black pepper

2 to 3 tablespoons sesame seeds, for garnish

2 cups cooked brown rice

FOR THE DRESSING

3 to 4 tablespoons tahini

2 tablespoons honey

1 lemon, juiced

1 garlic clove, minced

Salt

Freshly ground black pepper

1. Preheat the oven to 400°F. Spray two baking sheets with cooking spray.
2. Cover the first baking sheet with the broccoli and cauliflower and the second with the chickpeas and carrots. Toss each sheet with half of the oil and season with salt and pepper before placing in oven.
3. Cook the carrots and chickpeas for 10 minutes, leaving the carrots still just crisp, and the broccoli and cauliflower for 20 minutes, until tender. Stir each halfway through cooking.

4. To make the dressing, in a small bowl, mix the tahini, honey, lemon juice, and garlic. Season with salt and pepper and set aside.

5. Divide the rice into individual bowls, then layer with vegetables and drizzle dressing over the dish.

VARIATION TIP: *I usually add Brussels sprouts to this dish. You can blanch them whole, slice them in half, and roast with the rest of the vegetables in the oven.*

Per Serving Calories: 454; Protein: 12g; Total Carbohydrates: 62g; Sugars: 12g; Fiber: 11g; Total Fat: 18g; Saturated Fat: 3g; Cholesterol: 0mg; Sodium: 61mg

Quinoa with Almonds and Cranberries

**DAIRY-FREE,
GLUTEN-FREE,
VEGAN**

SERVES 4

PREP TIME:
15 minutes

This is a great lunch on the run. The creamy quinoa, sweet cranberries, and crunchy almonds play off each other and highlight one another's strengths nicely in this dish.

2 cups cooked quinoa

⅓ teaspoon cranberries or currants

¼ cup sliced almonds

2 garlic cloves, minced

1¼ teaspoons salt

½ teaspoon ground cumin

½ teaspoon turmeric

¼ teaspoon ground cinnamon

¼ teaspoon freshly ground black pepper

In a large bowl, toss the quinoa, cranberries, almonds, garlic, salt, cumin, turmeric, cinnamon, and pepper and stir to combine. Enjoy alone or with roasted cauliflower.

SUBSTITUTION TIP: *Feel free to use brown rice, freekeh, or wheat berries in place of quinoa for this dish.*

Per Serving Calories: 194; Protein: 7g; Total Carbohydrates: 31g; Sugars: <1g; Fiber: 4g; Total Fat: 6g; Saturated Fat: <1g; Cholesterol: 0mg; Sodium: 727mg

Mediterranean Baked Chickpeas

PREP TIME:
15 minutes

COOK TIME:
15 minutes

These chickpeas and tomatoes create a rich and creamy sauce that's divine over cauliflower rice or quinoa.

1 tablespoon extra-virgin olive oil

½ medium onion, chopped

3 garlic cloves, chopped

2 teaspoons smoked paprika

¼ teaspoon ground cumin

4 cups halved cherry tomatoes

2 (15-ounce) cans chickpeas, drained and rinsed

½ cup plain, unsweetened, full-fat Greek yogurt, for serving

1 cup crumbled feta, for serving

1. Preheat the oven to 425°F.
2. In an oven-safe sauté pan or skillet, heat the oil over medium heat and sauté the onion and garlic. Cook for about 5 minutes, until softened and fragrant. Stir in the paprika and cumin and cook for 2 minutes. Stir in the tomatoes and chickpeas.
3. Bring to a simmer for 5 to 10 minutes before placing in the oven.
4. Roast in oven for 25 to 30 minutes, until bubbling and thickened. To serve, top with Greek yogurt and feta.

SUBSTITUTION TIP: *You can use sour cream instead of Greek yogurt in a pinch.*

VARIATION TIP: *For a vegan version of this dish, skip the Greek yogurt and feta toppings.*

Per Serving Calories: 412; Protein: 20g; Total Carbohydrates: 51g; Sugars: 7g; Fiber: 13g; Total Fat: 15g; Saturated Fat: 7g; Cholesterol: 37mg; Sodium: 444mg

Falafel Bites

30 MINUTES OR LESS, DAIRY-FREE, GLUTEN-FREE, VEGAN

SERVES 4

PREP TIME:
15 minutes

COOK TIME:
15 minutes

These crunchy falafel bites are perfect to top a salad or wrap in a pita with lettuce, cucumbers, and some of the optional toppings below. Don't let me limit your falafel possibilities.

1⅔ cups falafel mix

1¼ cups water

Extra-virgin olive oil spray

1 tablespoon Pickled Onions (page 188) (optional)

1 tablespoon Pickled Turnips (page 187) (optional)

2 tablespoons Tzatziki Sauce (page 192) (optional)

1. In a large bowl, carefully stir the falafel mix into the water. Mix well. Let stand 15 minutes to absorb the water. Form mix into 1-inch balls and arrange on a baking sheet.
2. Preheat the broiler to high.
3. Take the balls and flatten slightly with your thumb (so they won't roll around on the baking sheet). Spray with olive oil, and then broil for 2 to 3 minutes on each side, until crispy and brown.
4. To fry the falafel, fill a pot with ½ inch of cooking oil and heat over medium-high heat to 375°F. Fry the balls for about 3 minutes, until brown and crisp. Drain on paper towels and serve with pickled onions, pickled turnips, and tzatziki sauce (if using).

INGREDIENT TIP: *It's really important to let the mix rest until the liquid is absorbed or else you won't be able to make patties that hold together.*

Per Serving Calories: 166; Protein: 17g; Total Carbohydrates: 30g; Sugars: 5g; Fiber: 8g; Total Fat: 2g; Saturated Fat: 0g; Cholesterol: 0mg; Sodium: 930mg

Quick Vegetable Kebabs

30 MINUTES OR LESS, DAIRY-FREE, GLUTEN-FREE, VEGAN

SERVES 4

PREP TIME:
15 minutes

COOK TIME:
15 minutes

This kebab is the only way I can get vegetables included in our family barbecues. The red pepper develops a great charred, sweet flavor. I can eat them like candy! It's important to note that some vegetables, such as carrots, potatoes, turnips, and other root vegetables, don't cook properly on a kebab skewer over the grill.

4 medium red onions, peeled and sliced into 6 wedges

4 medium zucchini, cut into 1-inch-thick slices

4 bell peppers, cut into 2-inch squares

2 yellow bell peppers, cut into 2-inch squares

2 orange bell peppers, cut into 2-inch squares

2 beefsteak tomatoes, cut into quarters

3 tablespoons Herbed Oil (page 184)

1. Preheat the oven or grill to medium-high or 350°F.
2. Thread 1 piece red onion, zucchini, different colored bell peppers, and tomatoes onto a skewer. Repeat until the skewer is full of vegetables, up to 2 inches away from the skewer end, and continue until all skewers are complete.
3. Put the skewers on a baking sheet and cook in the oven for 10 minutes or grill for 5 minutes on each side. The vegetables will be done with they reach your desired crunch or softness.
4. Remove the skewers from heat and drizzle with Herbed Oil.

LEFTOVER TIP: *Remove the vegetables from the skewers and throw them into a pita with some hummus for a quick lunch or dinner.*

PREP TIP: *If using wooden skewers, you will need to soak them for at least 30 minutes before threading vegetables to prevent scorching on the grill.*

Per Serving Calories: 240; Protein: 6g; Total Carbohydrates: 34g; Sugars: 15g; Fiber: 9g; Total Fat: 12g; Saturated Fat: 2g; Cholesterol: 0mg; Sodium: 38mg

Tortellini in Red Pepper Sauce

30 MINUTES OR LESS, VEGETARIAN

SERVES 4

PREP TIME:
15 minutes

COOK TIME:
10 minutes

The red pepper sauce plays nicely with the hearty tortellini pasta. I prefer fresh cheese tortellini for this recipe, but you can use whatever is most easily available to you. You can also try different tortellini fillings to find your favorite flavor combinations.

1 (16-ounce) container fresh cheese tortellini (usually green and white pasta)

1 (16-ounce) jar roasted red peppers, drained

1 teaspoon garlic powder

¼ cup tahini

1 tablespoon red pepper oil (optional)

1. Bring a large pot of water to a boil and cook the tortellini according to package directions.
2. In a blender, combine the red peppers with the garlic powder and process until smooth. Once blended, add the tahini until the sauce is thickened. If the sauce gets too thick, add up to 1 tablespoon red pepper oil (if using).
3. Once tortellini are cooked, drain and leave pasta in colander. Add the sauce to the bottom of the empty pot and heat for 2 minutes. Then, add the tortellini back into the pot and cook for 2 more minutes. Serve and enjoy!

VARIATION TIP: *For a low-carb or gluten-free version, try zucchini noodles in place of tortellini.*

Per Serving Calories: 350; Protein: 12g; Total Carbohydrates: 46g; Sugars: 2g; Fiber: 4g; Total Fat: 11g; Saturated Fat: 2g; Cholesterol: 44mg; Sodium: 192mg

Freekeh, Chickpea, and Herb Salad

30 MINUTES
OR LESS,
DAIRY-FREE,
GLUTEN-FREE,
VEGAN

**SERVES
4 TO 6**

PREP TIME:
15 minutes

COOK TIME:
10 minutes

The mint, parsley, and celery leaves in this dish create a light, airy salad that is full of fiber and protein. Sometimes I'll add in toasted walnuts for a nutty flavor.

1 (15-ounce) can chickpeas, rinsed and drained

1 cup cooked freekeh

1 cup thinly sliced celery

1 bunch scallions, both white and green parts, finely chopped

½ cup chopped fresh flat-leaf parsley

¼ cup chopped fresh mint

3 tablespoons chopped celery leaves

½ teaspoon kosher salt

⅓ cup extra-virgin olive oil

¼ cup freshly squeezed lemon juice

¼ teaspoon cumin seeds

1 teaspoon garlic powder

1. In a large bowl, combine the chickpeas, freekeh, celery, scallions, parsley, mint, celery leaves, and salt and toss lightly.
2. In a small bowl, whisk together the olive oil, lemon juice, cumin seeds, and garlic powder. Once combined, add to freekeh salad.

SUBSTITUTION TIP: *Feel free to swap in dried herbs in this dish; for instance, you can use 2 teaspoons of dried mint in place of the fresh ¼ cup.*

Per Serving Calories: 350; Protein: 9g; Total Carbohydrates: 38g; Sugars: 1g; Fiber: 9g; Total Fat: 19g; Saturated Fat: 2g; Cholesterol: 0mg; Sodium: 329mg

Kate's Warm Mediterranean Farro Bowl

30 MINUTES OR LESS, ONE PAN, VEGAN OPTION, VEGETARIAN

SERVES 4 TO 6

PREP TIME:
15 minutes

COOK TIME:
10 minutes

Packed with protein and fiber, farro is a great substitute for rice. This whole grain can be used in soups, salads, side dishes, and more. This dish marries whole-grain farro with an array of vegetables to create a hearty, filling, and nutrient-packed bowl.

⅓ cup extra-virgin olive oil

½ cup chopped red bell pepper

⅓ cup chopped red onions

2 garlic cloves, minced

1 cup zucchini, cut in ½-inch slices

½ cup canned chickpeas, drained and rinsed

½ cup coarsely chopped artichokes

3 cups cooked farro

Salt

Freshly ground black pepper

¼ cup sliced olives, for serving (optional)

½ cup crumbled feta cheese, for serving (optional)

2 tablespoons fresh basil, chiffonade, for serving (optional)

3 tablespoons balsamic reduction, for serving (optional)

1. In a large sauté pan or skillet, heat the oil over medium heat and sauté the pepper, onions, and garlic for about 5 minutes, until tender.
2. Add the zucchini, chickpeas, and artichokes, then stir and continue to sauté vegetables, approximately 5 more minutes, until just soft.
3. Stir in the cooked farro, tossing to combine and cooking enough to heat through. Season with salt and pepper and remove from the heat.

4. Transfer the contents of the pan into the serving vessels or bowls.

5. Top with olives, feta, and basil (if using). Drizzle with balsamic reduction (if using) to finish.

SUBSTITUTION TIP: *Swap out the farro for your favorite gluten-free base and turn this into the perfect gluten-free comfort dish. This versatile bowl can be served warm in the winter and fall or chilled in the summer and spring.*

Per Serving Calories: 367; Protein: 9g; Total Carbohydrates: 51g; Sugars: 2g; Fiber: 9g; Total Fat: 20g; Saturated Fat: 2g; Cholesterol: 0mg; Sodium: 87mg

Creamy Chickpea Sauce with Whole-Wheat Fusilli

VEGETARIAN

SERVES 4

PREP TIME:
15 minutes

COOK TIME:
20 minutes

The nutty, earthy flavor of the whole-grain pasta combined with the chickpeas creates a complete protein and balanced dish. I love it when flavors play nicely together, and this dish is no exception.

¼ cup extra-virgin olive oil

½ large shallot, chopped

5 garlic cloves, thinly sliced

1 (15-ounce) can chickpeas, drained and rinsed, reserving ½ cup canning liquid

Pinch red pepper flakes

1 cup whole-grain fusilli pasta

¼ teaspoon salt

⅛ teaspoon freshly ground black pepper

¼ cup shaved fresh Parmesan cheese

¼ cup chopped fresh basil

2 teaspoons dried parsley

1 teaspoon dried oregano

Red pepper flakes

1. In a medium pan, heat the oil over medium heat, and sauté the shallot and garlic for 3 to 5 minutes, until the garlic is golden. Add ¾ of the chickpeas plus 2 tablespoons of liquid from the can, and bring to a simmer.

2. Remove from the heat, transfer into a standard blender, and blend until smooth. At this point, add the remaining chickpeas. Add more reserved chickpea liquid if it becomes thick.

3. Bring a large pot of salted water to a boil and cook pasta until al dente, about 8 minutes. Reserve ½ cup of the pasta water, drain the pasta, and return it to the pot.

4. Add the chickpea sauce to the hot pasta and add up to ¼ cup of the pasta water. You may need to add more pasta water to reach your desired consistency.

5. Place the pasta pot over medium heat and mix occasionally until the sauce thickens. Season with salt and pepper.
6. Serve, garnished with Parmesan, basil, parsley, oregano, and red pepper flakes.

PREP TIP: *Make the sauce ahead of time for an easy assembly during weeknight dinner.*

Per Serving (1 cup pasta) Calories: 310; Protein: 10g; Total Carbohydrates: 33g; Sugars: 1g; Fiber: 7g; Total Fat: 17g; Saturated Fat: 3g; Cholesterol: 5mg; Sodium: 243mg

Linguine and Brussels Sprouts

ONE POT

SERVES 4

PREP TIME:
10 minutes

COOK TIME:
25 minutes

This is one of my favorite winter pastas. The wilted, savory Brussels sprouts become the vehicle for flavor in this dish.

8 ounces whole-wheat linguine

⅓ cup, plus 2 tablespoons extra-virgin olive oil, divided

1 medium sweet onion, diced

2 to 3 garlic cloves, smashed

8 ounces Brussels sprouts, chopped

½ cup chicken stock, as needed

⅓ cup dry white wine

½ cup shredded Parmesan cheese

1 lemon, cut in quarters

1. Bring a large pot of water to a boil and cook the pasta according to package directions. Drain, reserving 1 cup of the pasta water. Mix the cooked pasta with 2 tablespoons of olive oil, then set aside.
2. In a large sauté pan or skillet, heat the remaining ⅓ cup of olive oil on medium heat. Add the onion to the pan and cook for about 5 minutes, until softened. Add the smashed garlic cloves and cook for 1 minute, until fragrant.
3. Add the Brussels sprouts and cook covered for 15 minutes. Add chicken stock as needed to prevent burning. Once Brussels sprouts have wilted and are fork-tender, add white wine and cook down for about 7 minutes, until reduced.
4. Add the pasta to the skillet and add the pasta water as needed.
5. Serve with the Parmesan cheese and lemon for squeezing over the dish right before eating.

VARIATION TIP: *Sprinkle in some red pepper flakes while everything is cooking together for a punch of heat.*

Per Serving Calories: 502; Protein: 15g; Total Carbohydrates: 50g; Sugars: 3g; Fiber: 9g; Total Fat: 31g; Saturated Fat: 5g; Cholesterol: 10mg; Sodium: 246mg

Mozzarella and Sun-Dried Portobello Mushroom Pizza

30 MINUTES OR LESS, GLUTEN-FREE, VEGETARIAN

SERVES 4

PREP TIME:
10 minutes

COOK TIME:
10 minutes

If you wait to pull these out until the cheese bubbles through the sauce, you will not be sorry. The mushrooms will soften and take on the flavors of the cheese and sauce.

4 large portobello mushroom caps

3 tablespoons extra-virgin olive oil

Salt

Freshly ground black pepper

4 sun-dried tomatoes

1 cup mozzarella cheese, divided

½ to ¾ cup low-sodium tomato sauce

1. Preheat the broiler on high.
2. On a baking sheet, drizzle the mushroom caps with the olive oil and season with salt and pepper. Broil the portobello mushrooms for 5 minutes on each side, flipping once, until tender.
3. Fill each mushroom cap with 1 sun-dried tomato, 2 tablespoons of cheese, and 2 to 3 tablespoons of sauce. Top each with 2 tablespoons of cheese. Place the caps back under the broiler for a final 2 to 3 minutes, then quarter the mushrooms and serve.

VARIATION TIP: *Swap the tomato sauce for your favorite jarred pesto sauce to make a caprese mushroom cap. To satisfy any meat eaters in your family, throw ½ pound cooked, crumbed chicken sausage into the filling.*

Per Serving Calories: 218; Protein: 11g; Total Carbohydrates: 12g; Sugars: 3g; Fiber: 2g; Total Fat: 16g; Saturated Fat: 5g; Cholesterol: 15mg; Sodium: 244mg

Pesto and Roasted Pepper Pizza

VEGETARIAN

SERVES
5 TO 6

PREP TIME:
1 hour and
10 minutes
(1 hour
inactive)

COOK TIME:
20 minutes

I do a little happy dance whenever I make this because I know I get to have pizza the next day for lunch. The dough may look scary, but I promise you that after 2 or 3 doughs, you will have restaurant-quality pizza nights for an eighth of the price.

1½ cups warm water

1 teaspoon active dry yeast

¼ cup extra-virgin olive oil

2 tablespoons sugar

2 teaspoons kosher salt

4 cups all-purpose flour

10 ounces fresh mozzarella, shredded

⅓ cup pesto

⅓ cup chopped roasted red peppers

⅓ cup crumbled feta

1. In a small bowl, microwave the water for about 15 seconds, just until it's warm. Sprinkle the yeast into the warm water and let it stand for 10 minutes, until the top layer is foamy.
2. In a large bowl, whisk together the oil, sugar, and salt. Stir this into the yeast mix, then pour it back into the large bowl and add the flour.
3. Gently combine the flour mixture with a whisk or wooden spoon. Mix in the bowl until almost all the flour is incorporated and a ball of dough is formed. Cover the bowl with a heavy kitchen towel and let stand for 1 hour at room temperature.
4. Once the hour has passed, preheat the oven to 400°F and put a baking sheet upside-down in the oven.
5. Next, flour an area of the kitchen counter well and cut the pizza dough in half, reserving half for another pizza. Gently roll out half of the dough into a circle about 1 inch thick. The second half of the pizza dough will last for about 6 months in the freezer or 2 to 3 days in the refrigerator.

6. Reduce the heat to 375°F and remove the baking sheet from the oven. Place it upside-down on a heatproof surface. Place the pizza dough on the back of the hot baking sheet and put it in the oven for 5 to 7 minutes.

7. Remove the pizza from the oven and add mozzarella cheese first. Put it back into the oven and cook for 7 to 10 minutes. This will help dry out the wet, fresh mozzarella.

8. After 7 to 10 minutes, remove the pizza and add the pesto followed by the peppers and put it back into the oven for an additional 10 minutes.

9. Remove the pizza and let it rest for 5 minutes; while it's cooling, add the crumbled feta.

PREP TIP: *To save time, you can use store-bought dough instead of making your own.*

INGREDIENT TIP: *Don't make the water too hot; it will kill the yeast. The water should feel warm on the inside of your wrist.*

Per Serving Calories: 705; Protein: 23g; Total Carbohydrates: 78g; Sugars: 6g; Fiber: 3g; Total Fat: 32g; Saturated Fat: 12g; Cholesterol: 49mg; Sodium: 1,401mg

Lentil Burgers

30 MINUTES OR LESS, GLUTEN-FREE, VEGETARIAN

SERVES 4 TO 6

PREP TIME: 15 minutes

COOK TIME: 10 minutes

Welcome to the first veggie burger I ever mastered! This is a stress-free way to enjoy a savory, juicy burger without the cholesterol and saturated fat you'll get in a meat burger.

1 cup cooked green lentils, divided

½ cup plain, unsweetened, full-fat Greek yogurt

½ lemon, zested and juiced

½ teaspoon garlic powder, divided

⅛ teaspoon kosher salt, divided

6 ounces cremini mushrooms, finely chopped

3 tablespoons extra-virgin olive oil, divided

¼ teaspoon tablespoon white miso

¼ teaspoon smoked paprika

¼ cup gluten-free flour

1. In a blender, pour in ½ cup of lentils and partially puree until somewhat smooth, but with many whole lentils still remaining.
2. Meanwhile, in a small bowl, combine the yogurt, lemon zest and juice, ¼ teaspoon garlic powder, and half the salt. Season and set aside.
3. In a medium bowl, combine the mushrooms, 2 tablespoons of olive oil, miso, paprika, and the remaining ¼ teaspoon of garlic powder. Add all the lentils and stir. Vigorously stir in flour until the mixture holds together when squeezed; if it doesn't, continue to mash the lentils until it does and add 1 to 2 tablespoons flour if needed. Form into 6 patties about ¾ inch thick.

4. In a large nonstick sauté pan or skillet, working in batches, heat the remaining 1 tablespoon of olive oil over medium heat. Cook until the patties are deeply browned and very crisp on the bottom side, about 3 minutes. Carefully turn and repeat on second side, adding more oil as needed to maintain a light coating around patties in skillet. Repeat with remaining patties, adding more oil to the pan if needed.

5. Spread the reserved yogurt mixture into a pita. Top with patties and Pickled Onions (page 188).

Per Serving Calories: 216; Protein: 10g; Total Carbohydrates: 19g; Sugars: 3g; Fiber: 5g; Total Fat: 13g; Saturated Fat: 2g; Cholesterol: 4mg; Sodium: 69mg

Quick Seafood Paella, page 110

CHAPTER 8

Fish and Seafood Mains

Shrimp over Black Bean Linguine

30 MINUTES OR LESS, GLUTEN-FREE, ONE POT

SERVES 4

PREP TIME:
10 minutes

COOK TIME:
15 minutes

This is a frequent anniversary dinner that my husband and I make for each other. The black bean linguine is a play on the squid ink pastas you can get at high-end seafood restaurants.

1 pound black bean linguine or spaghetti

1 pound fresh shrimp, peeled and deveined

4 tablespoons extra-virgin olive oil

1 onion, finely chopped

3 garlic cloves, minced

¼ cup basil, cut into strips

1. Bring a large pot of water to a boil and cook the pasta according to the package instructions.
2. In the last 5 minutes of cooking the pasta, add the shrimp to the hot water and allow them to cook for 3 to 5 minutes. Once they turn pink, take them out of the hot water, and, if you think you may have overcooked them, run them under cool water. Set aside.
3. Reserve 1 cup of the pasta cooking water and drain the noodles. In the same pan, heat the oil over medium-high heat and cook the onion and garlic for 7 to 10 minutes. Once the onion is translucent, add the pasta back in and toss well.
4. Plate the pasta, then top with shrimp and garnish with basil.

SUBSTITUTION TIP: *Try swapping in jumbo lump crabmeat instead of shrimp for a different flavor and to save a cooking step.*

VARIATION TIP: *You can use your favorite pasta for this dish if you can't find black bean pasta.*

Per Serving Calories: 668; Protein: 57g; Total Carbohydrates: 73g; Sugars: 1g; Fiber: 31g; Total Fat: 19g; Saturated Fat: 2g; Cholesterol: 227mg; Sodium: 615mg

Easy Shrimp and Orzo Salad

30 MINUTES OR LESS

SERVES 4

PREP TIME:
10 minutes

COOK TIME:
10 minutes

The sweet crunch of the shrimp is balanced by the hearty whole-wheat orzo. I love to serve this dish warm over a bed of lettuce or alongside grilled vegetables.

1 cup orzo

1 hothouse cucumber, seeded and chopped

½ cup finely diced red onion

2 tablespoons extra-virgin olive oil

2 pounds (16- to 18-count) shrimp, peeled and deveined

3 lemons, juiced

Salt

Freshly ground black pepper

¾ cup crumbled feta cheese

2 tablespoons dried dill

1 cup chopped fresh flat-leaf parsley

1. Bring a large pot of water to a boil, then add the orzo. Cover, reduce heat, and simmer for 15 to 18 minutes, until the orzo is tender. Drain in a colander and set aside to cool.

2. In a separate bowl, combine the cucumber and red onion and set aside.

3. In a medium pan, heat the olive oil over medium heat. Add the shrimp. Reduce the heat and cook for 2 minutes on each side, or until fully cooked and pink.

4. Add the cooked shrimp to the bowl with the cucumber and onion, along with the lemon juice, and toss. Season with salt and pepper. Top with feta and dill, toss gently, and finish with parsley.

INGREDIENT TIP: *Cucumber peel can carry bitter undertones, so try peeling and seeding them for this dish. Try adding halved cherry tomatoes for even more flavor and color!*

Per Serving Calories: 567; Protein: 63g; Total Carbohydrates: 44g; Sugars: 5g; Fiber: 4g; Total Fat: 18g; Saturated Fat: 6g; Cholesterol: 505mg; Sodium: 2,226mg

Quick Seafood Paella

GLUTEN-FREE

SERVES 4

PREP TIME:
20 minutes

COOK TIME:
20 minutes

This dish is the embodiment of summer to me. My dad used to make this every Sunday night. The steaming paella would be passed around the table until it was so dark that we couldn't sit outside anymore.

¼ cup plus 1 tablespoon
extra-virgin olive oil

1 large onion,
finely chopped

2 tomatoes, peeled
and chopped

1½ tablespoons
garlic powder

1½ cups medium-grain
Spanish paella rice
or arborio rice

2 carrots, finely diced

Salt

1 tablespoon sweet paprika

8 ounces lobster meat
or canned crab

½ cup frozen peas

3 cups chicken stock,
plus more if needed

1 cup dry white wine

6 jumbo shrimp, unpeeled

⅓ pound calamari rings

1 lemon, halved

1. In a large sauté pan or skillet (16-inch is ideal), heat the oil over medium heat until small bubbles start to escape from oil. Add the onion and cook for about 3 minutes, until fragrant, then add tomatoes and garlic powder. Cook for 5 to 10 minutes, until the tomatoes are reduced by half and the consistency is sticky.

2. Stir in the rice, carrots, salt, paprika, lobster, and peas and mix well. In a pot or microwave-safe bowl, heat the chicken stock to almost boiling, then add it to the rice mixture. Bring to a simmer, then add the wine.

3. Smooth out the rice in the bottom of the pan. Cover and cook on low for 10 minutes, mixing occasionally, to prevent burning.

4. Top the rice with the shrimp, cover, and cook for 5 more minutes. Add additional broth to the pan if the rice looks dried out.

5. Right before removing the skillet from the heat, add the calamari rings. Toss the ingredients frequently. In about 2 minutes, the rings will look opaque. Remove the pan from the heat immediately—you don't want the paella to overcook). Squeeze fresh lemon juice over the dish.

VARIATION TIP: *If you have access to fresh seafood, you can add steamed clams to this dish for an extra punch.*

Per Serving Calories: 632; Protein: 34g; Total Carbohydrates: 71g; Sugars: 6g; Fiber: 5g; Total Fat: 20g; Saturated Fat: 3g; Cholesterol: 224mg; Sodium: 920mg

Fire-Roasted Salmon à l'Orange

DAIRY-FREE, GLUTEN-FREE

SERVES 4

PREP TIME:
10 minutes

COOK TIME:
25 minutes

This dish provides many layers of flavor, from the natural juices of the fish to the lovely spices. I hope you enjoy this dish as much and as often as our family does.

½ cup extra-virgin olive oil, divided

2 tablespoons balsamic vinegar

2 tablespoons garlic powder, divided

1 tablespoon cumin seeds

1 teaspoon sea salt, divided

1 teaspoon freshly ground black pepper, divided

2 teaspoons smoked paprika

4 (8-ounce) salmon fillets, skinless

2 small red onion, thinly sliced

½ cup halved Campari tomatoes

1 small fennel bulb, thinly sliced lengthwise

1 large carrot, thinly sliced

8 medium portobello mushrooms

8 medium radishes, sliced ⅛ inch thick

½ cup dry white wine

½ lime, zested

Handful cilantro leaves

½ cup halved pitted kalamata olives

1 orange, thinly sliced

4 roasted sweet potatoes, cut in wedges lengthwise

1. Preheat the oven to 375°F.
2. In a medium bowl, mix 6 tablespoons of olive oil, the balsamic vinegar, 1 tablespoon of garlic powder, the cumin seeds, ¼ teaspoon of sea salt, ¼ teaspoon of pepper, and the paprika. Put the salmon in the bowl and marinate while preparing the vegetables, about 10 minutes.
3. Heat an oven-safe sauté pan or skillet on medium-high heat and sear the top of the salmon for about 2 minutes, or until lightly brown. Set aside.

4. Add the remaining 2 tablespoons of olive oil to the same skillet. Once it's hot, add the onion, tomatoes, fennel, carrot, mushrooms, radishes, the remaining 1 teaspoon of garlic powder, ¾ teaspoon of salt, and ¾ teaspoon of pepper. Mix well and cook for 5 to 7 minutes, until fragrant. Add wine and mix well.

5. Place the salmon on top of the vegetable mixture, browned-side up. Sprinkle the fish with lime zest and cilantro and place the olives around the fish. Put orange slices over the fish and cook for about 7 additional minutes. While this is baking, add the sliced sweet potato wedges on a baking sheet and bake this alongside the skillet.

6. Remove from the oven, cover the skillet tightly, and let rest for about 3 minutes.

PREP TIP: *To reduce prep time, pre-blend the spices and precut the radishes, bulbs, and roasted peppers.*

Per Serving Calories: 841; Protein: 59g; Total Carbohydrates: 60g; Sugars: 15g; Fiber: 15g; Total Fat: 41g; Saturated Fat: 6g; Cholesterol: 170mg; Sodium: 908mg

Spicy Trout over Sautéed Mediterranean Salad

**DAIRY-FREE,
GLUTEN-FREE,
ONE PAN**

SERVES 4

PREP TIME:
10 minutes

COOK TIME:
30 minutes

This balanced, robust dish gets a touch of heat from the white pepper, and the veggies provide a flavorful base for the trout. This will surely become your new go-to seafood dinner.

2 pounds rainbow trout fillets (about 6 fillets)

Salt

Ground white pepper

1 tablespoon extra-virgin olive oil

1 pound asparagus

4 medium golden potatoes, thinly sliced

1 scallion, thinly sliced, green and white parts separated

1 garlic clove, finely minced

1 large carrot, thinly sliced

2 Roma tomatoes, chopped

8 pitted kalamata olives, chopped

¼ cup ground cumin

2 tablespoons dried parsley

2 tablespoons paprika

1 tablespoon vegetable bouillon seasoning

½ cup dry white wine

1. Lightly season the fish with salt and white pepper and set aside.
2. In a large sauté pan or skillet, heat the oil over medium heat. Add and stir in the asparagus, potatoes, the white part of the scallions, and garlic to the hot oil. Cook and stir for 5 minutes, until fragrant. Add the carrot, tomatoes, and olives; continue to cook for 5 to 7 minutes, until the carrots are slightly tender.
3. Sprinkle the cumin, parsley, paprika, and vegetable bouillon seasoning over the pan. Season with salt. Stir to incorporate. Put the trout on top of the vegetables and add the wine to cover the vegetables.

4. Reduce the heat to low, cover, and cook for 5 to 7 minutes, until the fish flakes easily with a fork and juices run clear. Top with scallion greens and serve.

INGREDIENT TIP: *This dish makes for a great leftover meal. Treat the fish with plenty of TLC so it doesn't fall apart during the storage and reheating process.*

Per Serving Calories: 493; Protein: 40g; Total Carbohydrates: 41g; Sugars: 8g; Fiber: 7g; Total Fat: 19g; Saturated Fat: 5g; Cholesterol: 110mg; Sodium: 736mg

Rosemary and Lemon Roasted Branzino

DAIRY-FREE, GLUTEN-FREE

SERVES 2

PREP TIME:
15 minutes

COOK TIME:
30 minutes

The tomatoes, kalamata olives, and carrot create an excellent contrast in this branzino dish. The rosemary adds an unmatchable aroma, especially while cooking. This is a dish for a lazy Sunday afternoon, so relax and enjoy. Taking a nap on the couch afterward is encouraged.

4 tablespoons extra-virgin olive oil, divided

2 (8-ounce) branzino fillets, preferably at least 1 inch thick

1 garlic clove, minced

1 bunch scallions, white part only, thinly sliced

½ cup sliced pitted kalamata or other good-quality black olives

1 large carrot, cut into ¼-inch rounds

10 to 12 small cherry tomatoes, halved

½ cup dry white wine

2 tablespoons paprika

2 teaspoons kosher salt

½ tablespoon ground chili pepper, preferably Turkish or Aleppo

2 rosemary sprigs or 1 tablespoon dried rosemary

1 small lemon, very thinly sliced

1. Warm a large, oven-safe sauté pan or skillet over high heat until hot, about 2 minutes. Carefully add 1 tablespoon of olive oil and heat until it shimmers, 10 to 15 seconds. Brown the branzino fillets for 2 minutes, skin-side up. Carefully flip the fillets skin-side down and cook for another 2 minutes, until browned. Set aside.

2. Swirl 2 tablespoons of olive oil around the skillet to coat evenly. Add the garlic, scallions, kalamata olives, carrot, and tomatoes, and let the vegetables sauté for 5 minutes, until softened. Add the wine, stirring until all ingredients are well integrated. Carefully place the fish over the sauce.

3. Preheat the oven to 450°F.

4. While the oven is heating, brush the fillets with 1 tablespoon of olive oil and season with paprika, salt, and chili pepper. Top each fillet with a rosemary sprig and several slices of lemon. Scatter the olives over fish and around the pan.

5. Roast until lemon slices are browned or singed, about 10 minutes.

INGREDIENT TIP: *Avoid olives that are soft or mushy. High-quality olives will maintain their texture during the cooking process.*

Per Serving Calories: 725; Protein: 58g; Total Carbohydrates: 25g; Sugars: 6g; Fiber: 10g; Total Fat: 43g; Saturated Fat: 7g; Cholesterol: 120mg; Sodium: 2,954mg

Crushed Marcona Almond Swordfish

GLUTEN-FREE

SERVES 4

PREP TIME:
25 minutes

COOK TIME:
15 minutes

Marcona almonds, a.k.a. the "Queen of Almonds," originate from Spain. They are sweeter and softer than other almond varieties. These sweeter and softer notes transform this dish into a crunchy, savory seafood experience.

½ cup almond flour

¼ cup crushed Marcona almonds

½ to 1 teaspoon salt, divided

2 pounds Swordfish, preferably 1 inch thick

1 large egg, beaten (optional)

¼ cup pure apple cider

¼ cup extra-virgin olive oil, plus more for frying

3 to 4 sprigs flat-leaf parsley, chopped

1 lemon, juiced

1 tablespoon Spanish paprika

5 medium baby portobello mushrooms, chopped (optional)

4 or 5 chopped scallions, both green and white parts

3 to 4 garlic cloves, peeled

¼ cup chopped pitted kalamata olives

1. On a dinner plate, spread the flour and crushed Marcona almonds and mix in the salt. Alternately, pour the flour, almonds, and ¼ teaspoon of salt into a large plastic food storage bag. Add the fish and coat it with the flour mixture. If a thicker coat is desired, repeat this step after dipping the fish in the egg (if using).
2. In a measuring cup, combine the apple cider, ¼ cup of olive oil, parsley, lemon juice, paprika, and ¼ teaspoon of salt. Mix well and set aside.

3. In a large, heavy-bottom sauté pan or skillet, pour the olive oil to a depth of ⅛ inch and heat on medium heat. Once the oil is hot, add the fish and brown for 3 to 5 minutes, then turn the fish over and add the mushrooms (If using), scallions, garlic, and olives. Cook for an additional 3 minutes. Once the other side of the fish is brown, remove the fish from the pan and set aside.

4. Pour the cider mixture into the skillet and mix well with the vegetables. Put the fried fish into the skillet on top of the mixture and cook with sauce on medium-low heat for 10 minutes, until the fish flakes easily with a fork. Carefully remove the fish from the pan and plate. Spoon the sauce over the fish. Serve with white rice or home-fried potatoes.

VARIATION TIP: *Try this dish with salmon, halibut, or sea bass fillet if swordfish isn't available. If you can't find Marcona almonds, try salted, unroasted almonds or walnuts.*

LEFTOVER TIP: *This fish goes great over a salad the next day.*

Per Serving Calories: 620; Protein: 63g; Total Carbohydrates: 10g; Sugars: 1g; Fiber: 5g; Total Fat: 37g; Saturated Fat: 6g; Cholesterol: 113mg; Sodium: 644mg

Cod à la Romana

GLUTEN-FREE

SERVES 2

PREP TIME:
15 minutes

COOK TIME:
25 minutes

This unassuming seafood dish receives depth from its stewed potatoes and kalamata olives. The acidity of the olives cuts through the dish and is highlighted by the artichoke hearts.

1-pound thick cod fillet, cut in 4 portions

¼ teaspoon paprika

¼ teaspoon onion powder (optional)

3 tablespoons extra-virgin olive oil

4 medium scallions

½ cup fresh chopped basil, divided

3 tablespoons minced garlic (optional)

2 teaspoons salt

2 teaspoons freshly ground black pepper

¼ teaspoon dry marjoram (optional)

6 sun-dried tomato slices

½ cup dry white wine

½ cup crumbled feta cheese

1 (15-ounce) can oil-packed artichoke hearts, drained

1 lemon, sliced

1 cup pitted kalamata olives

1 teaspoon capers (optional)

4 small red potatoes, quartered

1. Preheat the oven to 375°F.
2. Season the fish with paprika and onion powder (if using).
3. Heat an oven-safe sauté pan or skillet over medium heat and sear the top side of the cod for about 1 minute, or until golden. Set aside.
4. Pour the olive oil into the same skillet and heat over medium heat. Add the scallions, ¼ cup basil, garlic (if using), salt, pepper, marjoram (if using), tomatoes, and white wine and mix well. Bring to a boil and remove from heat.
5. Spread the sauce evenly on the bottom of pan. Then, evenly arrange the fish on top of the tomato basil sauce and sprinkle with feta cheese. Put the artichokes in the pan and top with lemon slices.

6. Sprinkle with olives, capers (if using), and the remaining ¼ cup of fresh basil. Remove from the stovetop and put in the pre-heated oven; bake the fish for 15 to 20 minutes, until it flakes easily with a fork.

7. Meanwhile, on a baking sheet or wrapped in aluminum foil, put the quartered potatoes in the oven and bake for 15 minutes, until fork-tender.

INGREDIENT TIP: *Fish is best enjoyed the same night it's cooked. If you think you may want to remake this delicious entrée later in the week, double the sauce for a fresh, stress-free weeknight dinner.*

VARIATION TIP: *If fish isn't your favorite protein, try this dish with 1 pound of shrimp and/or scallops. Shellfish tend to have a less "fishy" taste and are easy to work with.*

Per Serving Calories: 1,175; Protein: 64g; Total Carbohydrates: 94g; Sugars: 8g; Fiber: 13g; Total Fat: 60g; Saturated Fat: 11g; Cholesterol: 158mg; Sodium: 4,622mg

Braised Branzino over Scallions and Kalamata Olives

30 MINUTES OR LESS, DAIRY-FREE, GLUTEN-FREE

SERVES 2 TO 3

PREP TIME:
15 minutes

COOK TIME:
15 minutes

The combination of paprika, honey, and garlic releases an intoxicating aroma and incredible depth of flavor.

¾ cup dry white wine

2 tablespoons white wine vinegar

1 tablespoon honey

2 tablespoons cornstarch, divided

1 large branzino, butterflied

2 tablespoons paprika

2 tablespoons onion powder

½ tablespoon salt

6 tablespoons extra-virgin olive oil, divided

1 large tomato, cut into ¼-inch cubes

4 scallions, both green and white parts, thinly sliced

4 kalamata olives, pitted and chopped

4 garlic cloves, thinly sliced

1. In a bowl, combine the wine, vinegar, honey, and 2 teaspoons cornstarch, stirring until the honey has dissolved. Set aside.
2. Pat the fish very dry and put the fish skin-side down on a work surface. Sprinkle the fish with paprika, onion powder, and salt. Drizzle with 2 tablespoons of olive oil.
3. Preheat a large sauté pan or skillet over high heat until hot, about 2 minutes. Carefully add 2 tablespoons of olive oil and wait until it shimmers, 10 to 15 seconds. Brown the branzino, skin-side up, for about 2 minutes. Carefully flip it skin-side down and cook for another 2 minutes; set aside.

4. Swirl the remaining 2 tablespoons oil around skillet to evenly coat. Add the tomato, scallions, olives, and garlic and sauté for 5 minutes. Add the wine and vinegar mixture, stirring until all ingredients are well integrated. Carefully place the fish (skin-side down) over the sauce, reduce heat to medium-low, and cook for another 5 minutes. Transfer to a plate with a fork or slotted spoon.

LEFTOVER TIP: *This is a great leftover dish that I typically serve with roasted potatoes or steamed brown rice.*

Per Serving Calories: 1,060; Protein: 46g; Total Carbohydrates: 56g; Sugars: 14g; Fiber: 5g; Total Fat: 72g; Saturated Fat: 7g; Cholesterol: 90mg; Sodium: 2,808mg

Moroccan Crusted Sea Bass

**DAIRY-FREE,
GLUTEN-FREE**

SERVES 4

PREP TIME:
15 minutes

COOK TIME:
40 minutes

Sea bass offers a great canvas for the bold saffron, cumin, turmeric, herbs, and spices. The chickpeas soak up the juices and flavors from the sea bass.

1½ teaspoons ground turmeric, divided

¾ teaspoon saffron

½ teaspoon ground cumin

¼ teaspoon kosher salt

¼ teaspoon freshly ground black pepper

1½ pound sea bass fillets, about ½ inch thick

8 tablespoons extra-virgin olive oil, divided

8 garlic cloves, divided (4 minced cloves and 4 sliced)

6 medium baby portobello mushrooms, chopped

1 large carrot, sliced on an angle

2 sun-dried tomatoes, thinly sliced (optional)

2 tablespoons tomato paste

1 (15-ounce) can chickpeas, drained and rinsed

1½ cups low-sodium vegetable broth

¼ cup white wine

1 tablespoon ground coriander (optional)

1 cup sliced artichoke hearts marinated in olive oil

½ cup pitted kalamata olives

½ lemon, juiced

½ lemon, cut into thin rounds

4 to 5 rosemary sprigs or 2 tablespoons dried rosemary

Fresh cilantro, for garnish

1. In a small mixing bowl, combine 1 teaspoon turmeric and the saffron and cumin. Season with salt and pepper. Season both sides of the fish with the spice mixture. Add 3 tablespoons of olive oil and work the fish to make sure it's well coated with the spices and the olive oil.
2. In a large sauté pan or skillet, heat 2 tablespoons of olive oil over medium heat until shimmering but not smoking. Sear the top side of the sea bass for about 1 minute, or until golden. Remove and set aside.

3. In the same skillet, add the minced garlic and cook very briefly, tossing regularly, until fragrant. Add the mushrooms, carrot, sun-dried tomatoes (if using), and tomato paste. Cook for 3 to 4 minutes over medium heat, tossing frequently, until fragrant. Add the chickpeas, broth, wine, coriander (if using), and the sliced garlic. Stir in the remaining ½ teaspoon ground turmeric. Raise the heat, if needed, and bring to a boil, then lower heat to simmer. Cover part of the way and let the sauce simmer for about 20 minutes, until thickened.

4. Carefully add the seared fish to the skillet. Ladle a bit of the sauce on top of the fish. Add the artichokes, olives, lemon juice and slices, and rosemary sprigs. Cook another 10 minutes or until the fish is fully cooked and flaky. Garnish with fresh cilantro.

INGREDIENT TIP: *The juices created in this dish are best soaked up immediately. Serve with your favorite crusty bread, grain, or rice. Sea bass may be hard to find at your local fish counter. When this happens, I usually go for sablefish, otherwise known as black cod.*

Per Serving Calories: 696; Protein: 48g; Total Carbohydrates: 37g; Sugars: 3g; Fiber: 9g; Total Fat: 41g; Saturated Fat: 6g; Cholesterol: 90mg; Sodium: 810mg

Salmon Patties à la Puttanesca

30 MINUTES OR LESS

SERVES 2

PREP TIME:
10 minutes

COOK TIME:
20 minutes

This light and complex salmon patty is a great substitute for any meat-based burger. I enjoy this dish with a pita or whole-grain roll, pickled onions (page 188), and fresh lettuce leaves.

2 scallions, both white and green parts, thinly sliced

¼ cup light mayonnaise

3 tablespoons Dijon mustard

1 large egg, beaten

1 tablespoon freshly squeezed lemon juice

1 tablespoon dried parsley

1 teaspoon paprika

1 teaspoon red pepper flakes

½ tablespoon kosher salt

¼ teaspoon freshly ground black pepper

4 ounces fresh salmon (leftover salmon works well), finely diced

½ cup panko bread crumbs

2 tablespoons extra-virgin olive oil, plus more as needed

1. In a large bowl, combine the scallions, mayonnaise, mustard, egg, lemon juice, parsley, paprika, red pepper flakes, salt, and pepper and mix until well incorporated.
2. Add the salmon and panko bread crumbs to the bowl and combine. Form into 2 equal-size patties.
3. In a large sauté pan or skillet, heat the oil over medium heat. Cook the patties until golden and crispy, 3 to 4 minutes per side. Drain on paper towels.
4. Serve over spinach with lemon wedges, or stuff everything into a pita and enjoy!

SUBSTITUTION TIP: *If fresh salmon isn't available, this dish is great made with canned salmon. I recommend the brand Wild Planet; their canned seafood tastes so fresh.*

Per Serving Calories: 413; Protein: 18g; Total Carbohydrates: 25g; Sugars: 3g; Fiber: 2g; Total Fat: 25g; Saturated Fat: 3g; Cholesterol: 136mg; Sodium: 2559mg

Baked Spanish Salmon

30 MINUTES OR LESS, DAIRY-FREE

SERVES 4

PREP TIME:
10 minutes

COOK TIME:
20 minutes

The sweet taste of the red onion and carrots is perfectly balanced by the sharp flavor of fennel and stuffed olives.

2 small red onions, thinly sliced

1 cup shaved fennel bulbs

1 cup cherry tomatoes

15 green pimiento-stuffed olives

Salt

Freshly ground black pepper

1 teaspoon cumin seeds

½ teaspoon smoked paprika

4 (8-ounce) salmon fillets

½ cup low-sodium chicken broth

2 to 4 tablespoons extra-virgin olive oil

2 cups cooked couscous

1. Put the oven racks in the middle of the oven and preheat the oven to 375°F.
2. On 2 baking sheets, spread out the onions, fennel, tomatoes, and olives. Season them with salt, pepper, cumin, and paprika.
3. Place the fish over the vegetables, season with salt, and gently pour the broth over the 2 baking sheets. Drizzle a light stream of olive oil over baking sheets before popping them in the oven.
4. Bake the vegetables and fish for 20 minutes, checking halfway to ensure nothing is burning. Serve over couscous.

SUBSTITUTION TIP: *If salmon isn't available, try your next favorite hearty fish, like swordfish.*

LEFTOVER TIP: *Use any leftover salmon you may have for the Salmon Patties à la Puttanesca (page 126).*

Per Serving Calories: 476; Protein: 50g; Total Carbohydrates: 26g; Sugars: 3g; Fiber: 3g; Total Fat: 18g; Saturated Fat: 3g; Cholesterol: 170mg; Sodium: 299mg

Chicken Kebabs with Tzatziki Sauce, page 144

Poultry Mains

Chicken Cacciatore

**DAIRY-FREE,
ONE PAN**

SERVES
4 TO 6

PREP TIME:
20 minutes

COOK TIME:
1 hour and
10 minutes

This was the first dish my mother-in-law taught me how to make. I was all nerves while prepping, but as the flavors started to develop, it was apparent that what we were making would be delicious! I breathed a sigh of relief when I took my first bite.

2 tablespoons extra-virgin olive oil

½ cup diced carrots

2 garlic cloves, minced

½ cup chopped celery

2 onions, chopped

2 pounds chicken tenders

2 (14.5-ounce) cans Italian seasoned diced tomatoes, drained

2 cups cooked corkscrew pasta, such as whole-grain fusilli

1. In a large saucepan, heat the oil over medium-high heat and sauté the carrots, garlic, celery, and onions for about 5 minutes, until softened. Add the chicken and brown for 4 to 5 minutes on each side.

2. Add the diced tomatoes. Cover and reduce heat to simmer for an hour. Serve over pasta.

INGREDIENT TIP: *If you find the chicken too dry or tough, you can tenderize it more with a meat mallet.*

VARIATION TIP: *Use gluten-free pasta for a gluten-free version of this dish.*

Per Serving Calories: 416; Protein: 58g; Total Carbohydrates: 38g; Sugars: 9g; Fiber: 7g; Total Fat: 3g; Saturated Fat: 0g; Cholesterol: 130mg; Sodium: 159mg

Rosemary Baked Chicken Thighs

DAIRY-FREE, GLUTEN-FREE, ONE PAN

SERVES 4 TO 6

PREP TIME: 20 minutes

COOK TIME: 20 minutes

Let the aromas of this dish fill your house and push away any stressors dragged in from work. This dish checks all the boxes: juicy, flavorful, and easy.

5 tablespoons extra-virgin olive oil, divided

3 medium shallots, diced

4 garlic cloves, peeled and crushed

1 rosemary sprig

2 to 2½ pounds bone-in, skin-on chicken thighs (about 6 pieces)

2 teaspoons kosher salt

¼ teaspoon freshly ground black pepper

1 lemon, juiced and zested

⅓ cup low-sodium chicken broth

1. In a large sauté pan or skillet, heat 3 tablespoons of olive oil over medium heat. Add the shallots and garlic and cook for about a minute, until fragrant. Add the rosemary sprig.
2. Season the chicken with salt and pepper. Place it in the skillet, skin-side down, and brown for 3 to 5 minutes.
3. Once it's cooked halfway through, turn the chicken over and add lemon juice and zest.
4. Add the chicken broth, cover the pan, and continue to cook for 10 to 15 more minutes, until cooked through and juices run clear. Serve.

PREP TIP: *Prep the shallots and garlic ahead of time to reduce chopping time while assembling this meal.*

Per Serving Calories: 683; Protein: 39g; Total Carbohydrates: 9g; Sugars: 2g; Fiber: 1g; Total Fat: 56g; Saturated Fat: 13g; Cholesterol: 222mg; Sodium: 1,174mg

Southward Pesto Stuffed Peppers

GLUTEN-FREE

> SERVES
> 4 TO 6

PREP TIME:
20 minutes

COOK TIME:
15 minutes

Ground lean meats like turkey and chicken pack protein and flavor and can be used in a variety of dishes. Ground meats are often cost-effective as well. Substituting ground meat in place of added rice, breading, or other starch makes this dish nutrient-packed and filling without all the added carbohydrates. Easy to prepare, this can be a fun dish that the whole family can take part in making and enjoying.

Nonstick cooking spray

3 large bell peppers, halved

2 tablespoons extra-virgin olive oil, plus more to garnish

¼ cup cooked chickpeas

½ shredded carrot

2 garlic cloves, minced

1 pound ground turkey or chicken

Salt

Freshly ground black pepper

1 cup cooked brown rice

½ cup halved cherry tomatoes

½ zucchini, chopped

1 tablespoon dried Italian herb medley

2 tablespoons chopped black olives

6 tablespoons prepared pesto

½ cup shredded Italian cheese blend

1. Preheat the oven to 350°F. Lightly spray a medium-size casserole or glass baking dish with cooking spray.
2. Bring a medium pot of water to a boil and reduce to a steady simmer. Using tongs to lower the peppers in the water, simmer each pepper half for about 3 minutes, just to soften. Remove from the water and drain in a colander.
3. In a large sauté pan or skillet, heat the olive oil over medium-high heat and sauté the chickpeas and carrot for about 5 minutes, until tender. Add the garlic and sauté for 1 minute, until fragrant. Then add the turkey, season with salt and pepper, and toss to cook evenly.

4. Just before the turkey is cooked through, add the rice, cherry tomatoes, zucchini, and herbs, and sauté an additional 5 to 7 minutes, until cooked through.
5. Remove from the heat and stir in the olives. Place the prepared pepper halves in the greased casserole dish.
6. Divide the filling evenly among the peppers. Top each pepper with 1 tablespoon of pesto and a sprinkle of Italian cheese. Bake the peppers for 7 to 10 minutes, until heated through. Allow the peppers to rest for 10 minutes before serving. Drizzle with a dash of your favorite olive oil and enjoy!

VARIATION TIP: *There are a variety of different pesto sauces, from traditional to nut-free and dairy-free. Feel free to substitute with your favorite red sauce or light Italian dressing for a twist on the flavor as well.*

Per Serving Calories: 546; Protein: 26g; Total Carbohydrates: 28g; Sugars: 5g; Fiber: 5g; Total Fat: 38g; Saturated Fat: 11g; Cholesterol: 110mg; Sodium: 493mg

Spanish-Seasoned Chicken and Rice

DAIRY-FREE, GLUTEN-FREE

SERVES 2

PREP TIME:
15 minutes

COOK TIME:
30 minutes

This is a simple and delicious dish that's ready in less than an hour. The paprika gives a richness and depth that's surprising and warming at the same time.

2 teaspoons smoked paprika

2 teaspoons ground cumin

1½ teaspoons garlic salt

¾ teaspoon chili powder

¼ teaspoon dried oregano

1 lemon

2 boneless, skinless chicken breasts

3 tablespoons extra-virgin olive oil, divided

2 large shallots, diced

1 cup uncooked white rice

2 cups vegetable stock

1 cup broccoli florets

⅓ cup chopped parsley

1. In a small bowl, whisk together the paprika, cumin, garlic salt, chili powder, and oregano. Divide in half and set aside. Into another small bowl, juice the lemon and set aside.
2. Put the chicken in a medium bowl. Coat the chicken with 2 tablespoons of olive oil and rub with half of the seasoning mix.
3. In a large pan, heat the remaining 1 tablespoon of olive oil and cook the chicken for 2 to 3 minutes on each side, until just browned but not cooked through.
4. Add shallots to the same pan and cook until translucent, then add the rice and cook for 1 more minute to toast. Add the vegetable stock, lemon juice, and the remaining seasoning mix and stir to combine. Return the chicken to the pan on top of the rice. Cover and cook for 15 minutes.

5. Uncover and add the broccoli florets. Cover and cook an additional 5 minutes, until the liquid is absorbed, rice is tender, and chicken is cooked through.
6. Top with freshly chopped parsley and serve immediately.

VARIATION TIP: *Use 3 chicken thighs in place of breasts for a slightly higher-calorie, juicer version.*

Per Serving Calories: 750; Protein: 36g; Total Carbohydrates: 101g; Sugars: 10g; Fiber: 7g; Total Fat: 25g; Saturated Fat: 4g; Cholesterol: 65mg; Sodium: 1,823mg

Tricolored Spanish Chicken and Artichokes

DAIRY-FREE

SERVES 2

PREP TIME:
15 minutes

COOK TIME:
25 minutes

This is a hearty meal I like to make on cold fall nights. The seasoned wheatberries balance the chicken and the Spanish olives add a nice depth to the rice, enhancing the overall flavor of this dish.

1½ cups chicken stock

1 cup wheatberries

3 tablespoons extra-virgin olive oil, divided

1 (9-ounce) package frozen artichoke hearts, chopped

2 roasted red peppers, jarred in oil, finely chopped

⅓ cup chopped pitted Spanish green olives

2 (6-ounce) boneless, skinless chicken breasts

½ teaspoon salt, divided

½ teaspoon freshly ground black pepper, divided

½ cup whole-grain all-purpose flour

½ tablespoon smoked paprika

2 large eggs

½ cup panko bread crumbs

½ cup chopped flat-leaf parsley

¼ teaspoon garlic powder

¼ teaspoon onion powder

1. In a pot, bring the stock to a boil. Stir in the wheatberries and 1 tablespoon of olive oil. Cover and reduce the heat to low and cook for 20 minutes.
2. Add the artichokes, peppers, and olives and stir to combine. Cover and cook for 5 minutes more, turn off the heat, and fluff with a fork. Check the wheatberries for desired texture. They should be chewy but not tough. There should be minimal to no water in the pot when done.
3. In a large sauté pan or skillet, heat the remaining 2 tablespoons of olive oil over low heat.
4. Butterfly the chicken breasts by slicing them almost in half starting at the thickest part. (Don't cut all the way through!) Open each chicken breast and season both the inside and outside with ¼ teaspoon of salt and ¼ teaspoon of pepper.

5. On a plate, blend together the flour, smoked paprika, remaining ¼ teaspoon of salt, and remaining ¼ teaspoon of pepper. In a separate bowl, beat eggs. Prepare a third plate with panko, parsley, garlic powder, and onion powder.

6. Dredge the chicken first in flour mixture, then in the egg, and finally in the panko.

7. Raise the heat of the pan with the olive oil to medium-high. When the oil is hot, using tongs to flip, brown the chicken on both sides. Reduce the heat and cover the pan. Cook for 10 more minutes, or until cooked through and juices run clear.

SUBSTITUTION TIP: *For Mediterranean chicken wings, try this recipe with skinless chicken thighs and wings.*

Per Serving Calories: 1,094; Protein: 67g; Total Carbohydrates: 127g; Sugars: 5g; Fiber: 31g; Total Fat: 40g; Saturated Fat: 7g; Cholesterol: 284mg; Sodium: 1,652mg

Lemony Chicken over Sautéed Vegetables

GLUTEN-FREE

SERVES 4

PREP TIME:
55 minutes

COOK TIME:
45 minutes

The mushrooms, carrots, and zucchini offer complexity and depth to this chicken dinner, but sometimes I like to swap out the vegetables. You can also try it with artichoke hearts or Brussels sprouts.

6 tablespoons extra-virgin olive oil, divided

4 large garlic cloves, crushed

1 tablespoon dried basil

1 tablespoon dried parsley

1 tablespoon salt

½ tablespoon thyme

4 skin-on, bone-in chicken thighs

6 medium portobello mushrooms, quartered

1 large zucchini, sliced

1 large carrot thinly sliced

⅛ cup pitted kalamata olives

8 pieces sun-dried tomatoes (optional)

½ cup dry white wine

1 lemon, sliced

1. In a small bowl, combine 4 tablespoons of olive oil, the garlic cloves, basil, parsley, salt, and thyme. Store half of the marinade in a jar and, in a bowl, combine the remaining half to marinate the chicken thighs for about 30 minutes.
2. Preheat the oven to 430°F.
3. In a large skillet or oven-safe pan, heat the remaining 2 tablespoons of olive oil over medium-high heat. Sear the chicken for 3 to 5 minutes on each side until golden brown, and set aside.
4. In the same pan, sauté portobello mushrooms, zucchini, and carrot for about 5 minutes, or until lightly browned.
5. Add the chicken thighs, olives, and sun-dried tomatoes (if using). Pour the wine over the chicken thighs.
6. Cover the pan and cook for about 10 minutes over medium-low heat.

7. Uncover the pan and transfer it to the oven. Cook for 15 more minutes, or until the chicken skin is crispy and the juices run clear. Top with lemon slices.

INGREDIENT TIP: *Make sure to remove any excess skin when prepping the chicken. Also, in an effort to eliminate the water trapped in the zucchini, onions, and bell pepper, sauté them before adding the chicken and putting it in the oven. This will allow the chicken to crisp and the vegetables to maintain their flavor.*

Per Serving Calories: 544; Protein: 28g; Total Carbohydrates: 20g; Sugars: 5g; Fiber: 11g; Total Fat: 41g; Saturated Fat: 8g; Cholesterol: 111mg; Sodium: 1,848mg

Sweet and Savory Stuffed Chicken

30 MINUTES OR LESS, GLUTEN-FREE

SERVES 4

PREP TIME:
10 minutes

COOK TIME:
20 minutes

The sweet-and-spicy nature of the dish, from the apricots and harissa, is a welcome change to humdrum grilled chicken. The stuffing stays juicy throughout the cooking process.

⅓ cup cooked brown rice

1 teaspoon Shawarma Spice Rub (page 162)

4 (6-ounce) boneless skinless chicken breasts

1 tablespoon harissa

3 tablespoons extra-virgin olive oil, divided

Salt

Freshly ground black pepper

4 small dried apricots, halved

⅓ cup crumbled feta

1 tablespoon chopped fresh parsley

1. Preheat the oven to 375°F.
2. In a medium bowl, mix the rice and shawarma seasoning and set aside.
3. Butterfly the chicken breasts by slicing them almost in half, starting at the thickest part and folding them open like a book.
4. In a small bowl, mix the harissa with 1 tablespoon of olive oil. Brush the chicken with the harissa oil and season with salt and pepper. The harissa adds a nice heat, so feel free to add a thicker coating for more spice.
5. Onto one side of each chicken breast, spoon 1 to 2 tablespoons of rice, then layer 2 apricot halves in each breast. Divide the feta between the chicken breasts and fold the other side over the filling to close.
6. In an oven-safe sauté pan or skillet, heat the remaining 2 tablespoons of olive oil and sear the breast for 2 minutes on each side, then place the pan into the oven for 15 minutes, or until fully cooked and juices run clear. Serve, garnished with parsley.

VARIATION TIP: *Try skinless chicken thighs if breast is not available.*

LEFTOVER TIP: *The stuffing in the chicken breast tends to dry out overnight in the refrigerator, but you can reheat it the next day with a drizzle of prepared pesto to add moisture.*

Per Serving Calories: 321; Protein: 37g; Total Carbohydrates: 8g; Sugars: 3g; Fiber: 1g; Total Fat: 17g; Saturated Fat: 4g; Cholesterol: 109mg; Sodium: 410mg

Spinach and Feta Stuffed Chicken

ONE PAN

PREP TIME:
10 minutes

COOK TIME:
25 minutes

This chicken dinner makes me think of September and the beginning of fall. Stuffing the chicken with spinach is a great way to get your vegetables.

4 tablespoons extra-virgin olive oil, divided

½ cup chopped shallots

1 lemon, zested and juiced

1 garlic clove, minced

⅓ cup chopped baby spinach

½ cup crumbled feta cheese

4 finely chopped pitted kalamata olives

Salt

Freshly ground black pepper

2 boneless, skinless chicken breasts

2 teaspoons whole-wheat flour

1. Preheat the oven to 350°F.
2. In an oven-safe, nonstick sauté pan or skillet, heat 2 tablespoons of olive oil over medium heat until it shimmers. Add the shallots and cook for 3 to 5 minutes, until translucent. Add the lemon zest and juice and garlic and heat for about 1 minute, until fragrant.
3. Add the spinach and stir for 3 to 5 minutes, until heated through and most of the water is cooked out of the spinach. Transfer the spinach-shallot mixture to a bowl. Wipe the skillet clean and set aside. Stir the feta cheese and olives into the spinach mixture. Season with salt and pepper.
4. Butterfly the chicken breasts by slicing them almost in half, starting at the thickest part, and folding them open like a book. Make sure not to cut all the way through. Season with salt and pepper.
5. Onto one side of each chicken breast, place half of the shallot and spinach mixture and fold the other side over the filling to close. Use toothpicks to hold the sides together. Dust the chicken lightly with flour, salt, and pepper.

6. Return the skillet to high heat and sear the stuffed chicken for 2 minutes on each side. If the pan looks dry, add the remaining 2 tablespoons of olive oil to the pan while it's cooking. Once all sides are seared, put the pan in the oven.

7. Bake for 15 to 20 minutes, or until the breasts are cooked through and juices run clear.

VARIATION TIP: *Try blue cheese instead of feta for a bolder, more robust flavor profile.*

Per Serving Calories: 513; Protein: 30g; Total Carbohydrates: 15g; Sugars: 5g; Fiber: 3g; Total Fat: 41g; Saturated Fat: 10g; Cholesterol: 98mg; Sodium: 731mg

Chicken Kebabs with Tzatziki Sauce

**DAIRY-FREE,
GLUTEN-FREE**

SERVES 2

PREP TIME:
45 minutes

COOK TIME:
20 minutes

The marinade gives this chicken dish notes of authentic Mediterranean seasonings. The vegetable swap-ins are endless and can be adjusted based on your tastes. If you're using wooden skewers, be sure to soak them for at least half an hour so they don't burn.

**½ cup extra-virgin
olive oil, divided**

½ large lemon, juiced

2 garlic cloves, minced

**½ teaspoon
za'atar seasoning**

Salt

**Freshly ground
black pepper**

**1 pound boneless skinless
chicken breasts, cut
into 1¼-inch cubes**

**1 large red bell pepper,
cut into 1¼-inch pieces**

**2 small zucchini (nearly
1 pound), cut into rounds
slightly under ½ inch thick**

**2 large shallots, diced
into quarters**

Tzatziki Sauce (page 192)

1. In a bowl, whisk together ⅓ cup of olive oil, lemon juice, garlic, za'atar, salt, and pepper.

2. Put the chicken in a medium bowl and pour the olive oil mixture over the chicken. Press the chicken into the marinade. Cover and refrigerate for 45 minutes. While the chicken marinates, soak the wooden skewers in water for 30 minutes.

3. Drizzle and toss the pepper, zucchini, and shallots with the remaining 2½ tablespoons of olive oil and season lightly with salt.

4. Preheat the oven to 500°F and put a baking sheet in the oven to heat.

5. On each skewer, thread a red bell pepper, zucchini, shallot and 2 chicken pieces and repeat twice. Put the kebabs onto the hot baking sheet and cook for 7 to 9 minutes, or until the chicken is cooked through. Rotate once halfway through cooking. Serve the kebabs warm with the Tzatziki Sauce.

SUBSTITUTION TIP: *If you do not have za'atar seasoning, you can add ¼ teaspoon of dried thyme, ¼ teaspoon of dried oregano, and ¼ teaspoon of ground coriander for a similar flavor profile.*

INGREDIENT TIP: *Do not marinate the dish for more than an hour; the acidity will make the chicken soft.*

Per Serving (2 kebabs each without Tzatziki) Calories: 825; Protein: 51g; Total Carbohydrates: 31g; Sugars: 13g; Fiber: 5g; Total Fat: 59g; Saturated Fat: 8g; Cholesterol: 130mg; Sodium: 379mg

Moroccan Meatballs

DAIRY-FREE

**SERVES
4 TO 6**

PREP TIME:
10 minutes

COOK TIME:
10 minutes

The chicken acts as a vehicle for all the flavors in this dish to get into your mouth! The paprika, garlic powder, cardamom, and parsley shine through nicely.

2 large shallots, diced

2 tablespoons finely chopped parsley

2 teaspoons paprika

1 teaspoon ground cumin

½ teaspoon ground coriander

½ teaspoon garlic powder

½ teaspoon salt

½ teaspoon freshly ground black pepper

⅛ teaspoon ground cardamom

1 pound ground chicken

½ cup all-purpose flour, to coat

¼ cup olive oil, divided

1. In a bowl, combine the shallots, parsley, paprika, cumin, coriander, garlic powder, salt, pepper, and cardamom. Mix well.
2. Add the chicken to the spice mixture and mix well. Form into 1-inch balls flattened to about ½-inch thickness.
3. Put the flour in a bowl for dredging. Dip the balls into the flour until coated.
4. Pour enough oil to cover the bottom of a sauté pan or skillet and heat over medium heat. Working in batches, cook the meatballs, turning frequently, for 2 to 3 minutes on each side, until they are cooked through. Add more oil between batches as needed. Serve in a pita, topped with lettuce dressed with Cider Yogurt Dressing (page 194).

PREP TIP: *Blend herbs during the weekend prep day for a stress-free, flavorful weeknight meatball dinner.*

Per Serving Calories: 405; Protein: 24g; Total Carbohydrates: 20g; Sugars:3g; Fiber: 1g; Total Fat: 26g; Saturated Fat: 5g; Cholesterol: 95mg; Sodium: 387mg

Greek Chicken Burgers

30 MINUTES OR LESS

SERVES 4

PREP TIME:
10 minutes

COOK TIME:
10 minutes

These burgers are diverse in flavor and as easy to make as traditional burgers. Try them in a pita topped with Pickled Turnips (page 187) and Spicy Cucumber Dressing.

1 pound ground chicken

¼ cup finely chopped red onion

3 tablespoons finely chopped red pepper

3 tablespoons crumbled feta cheese

3 tablespoons panko bread crumbs

1 garlic clove, minced

1 teaspoon chopped fresh oregano

¼ teaspoon salt

⅛ teaspoon freshly ground black pepper

Pita bread, for serving

Pickled Onions (page 188), for serving

Hummus, for serving

1. In a large bowl, combine the chicken, onion, peppers, feta, panko, garlic, oregano, salt, and pepper. Mix well and shape into 8 patties.
2. Preheat a grill to medium-high.
3. Grill the burgers for 4 to 5 minutes on each side, until the juices run clear and the patty is cooked through. Serve on pita topped with pickled onions and hummus.

LEFTOVER TIP: *Dice up any leftovers and toss them into your favorite salad.*

VARIATION TIP: *To make on the stovetop, heat a nonstick skillet over medium-high heat and cook for 4 to 5 minutes on each side, until cooked through.*

Per Serving Calories: 242; Protein: 23g; Total Carbohydrates: 7g; Sugars: 1g; Fiber: 1g; Total Fat: 14g; Saturated Fat: 4g; Cholesterol: 101mg; Sodium: 322mg

Savory Chicken Meatballs

GLUTEN-FREE

SERVES 4

PREP TIME:
20 minutes

COOK TIME:
20 minutes

The shallots start this dish off on a sweet note and the feta offers the tangy balance needed to make this patty an all-star addition to your weekly recipe rotation.

2 (1-pound) boxes frozen chopped spinach, thawed

1 medium shallot, grated

1 pound ground chicken

¾ cup crumbled feta cheese

2 tablespoons za'atar seasoning

¼ cup extra-virgin olive oil

4 whole-wheat pita bread rounds, for serving

Tzatziki Sauce (page 192), for serving

⅓ seedless cucumber, peeled and chopped, for serving

1. Preheat the oven to 400°F.
2. While the oven preheats, squeeze all the water out of the spinach until it's completely dry. Use paper towels to blot it if necessary.
3. In a bowl, fluff the spinach with a fork to separate clumps and add the grated shallot to the spinach. Add the chicken, feta, and za'atar seasoning to the spinach and shallots and drizzle with the olive oil.
4. Combine all the ingredients and form the mixture into 10 to 15 meatballs. Lightly flatten the meatballs (just so that they won't roll around) and place on a nonstick baking sheet.
5. Bake for 10 to 12 minutes, or until the meatballs are golden brown and cooked thoroughly.
6. Serve in a pita, topped with Tzatziki Sauce and cucumbers.

SUBSTITUTION TIP: *Don't have za'atar seasoning for this chicken? Your favorite grill seasoning will work as a snappy replacement.*

Per Serving Calories: 642; Protein: 39g; Total Carbohydrates: 53g; Sugars: 5g; Fiber: 13g; Total Fat: 34g; Saturated Fat: 9g; Cholesterol: 120mg; Sodium: 896mg

Mediterranean Lamb Bowl, page 152

Meat Mains

Mediterranean Lamb Bowl

30 MINUTES OR LESS, GLUTEN-FREE, ONE PAN

SERVES 2

PREP TIME:
15 minutes

COOK TIME:
15 minutes

You can't get bored with this dish, because it's so simple to update. The version outlined below is my take on this weekday staple. The hummus makes this dish feel more substantial, but if you want a lighter meal, try Tzatziki Sauce (page 192).

2 tablespoons extra-virgin olive oil

¼ cup diced yellow onion

1 pound ground lamb

1 teaspoon dried mint

1 teaspoon dried parsley

½ teaspoon red pepper flakes

¼ teaspoon garlic powder

1 cup cooked rice

½ teaspoon za'atar seasoning

½ cup halved cherry tomatoes

1 cucumber, peeled and diced

1 cup store-bought hummus or Garlic-Lemon Hummus (page 76)

1 cup crumbled feta cheese

2 pita breads, warmed (optional)

1. In a large sauté pan or skillet, heat the olive oil over medium heat and cook the onion for about 2 minutes, until fragrant. Add the lamb and mix well, breaking up the meat as you cook. Once the lamb is halfway cooked, add mint, parsley, red pepper flakes, and garlic powder.

2. In a medium bowl, mix together the cooked rice and za'atar, then divide between individual serving bowls. Add the seasoned lamb, then top the bowls with the tomatoes, cucumber, hummus, feta, and pita (if using).

SUBSTITUTION TIP: *If you don't have za'atar seasoning, try seasoning the rice with ¼ teaspoon of dried ginger, cumin, and turmeric for a lighter flavor.*

Per Serving Calories: 1,312; Protein: 62g; Total Carbohydrates: 62g; Sugars: 7g; Fiber: 12g; Total Fat: 96g; Saturated Fat: 39g; Cholesterol: 232mg; Sodium: 1,454mg

Lamb Burger

30 MINUTES OR LESS, DAIRY-FREE, GLUTEN-FREE

SERVES 4

PREP TIME:
15 minutes

COOK TIME:
15 minutes

This recipe came about from complete boredom with the typical beef patty. I love that Mediterranean cooking sneaks vegetables into its dishes, and this one is no exception. The red onion keeps the burger moist and adds acidity to brighten up the patty.

1 pound ground lamb

½ small red onion, grated

1 tablespoon dried parsley

1 teaspoon dried oregano

1 teaspoon ground cumin

1 teaspoon garlic powder

½ teaspoon dried mint

¼ teaspoon paprika

¼ teaspoon kosher salt

⅛ teaspoon freshly ground black pepper

Extra-virgin olive oil, for panfrying

4 pita breads, for serving (optional)

Tzatziki Sauce (page 192), for serving (optional)

Pickled Onions (page 188), for serving (optional)

1. In a bowl, combine the lamb, onion, parsley, oregano, cumin, garlic powder, mint, paprika, salt, and pepper. Divide the meat into 4 small balls and work into smooth discs.
2. In a large sauté pan or skillet, heat a drizzle of olive oil over medium heat or brush a grill with oil and set it to medium. Cook the patties for 4 to 5 minutes on each side, until cooked through and juices run clear.
3. Enjoy lamb burgers in pitas, topped with tzatziki sauce and pickled onions (if using).

PREP TIP: *You can make this mix up to 1 day in advance. The meat may turn a grayish color, but that's from the meat oxidizing in the container.*

Per Serving Calories: 328; Protein: 19g; Total Carbohydrates: 2g; Sugars: 1g; Fiber: 1g; Total Fat: 27g; Saturated Fat: 12g; Cholesterol: 83mg; Sodium: 215mg

Quick Herbed Lamb and Pasta

GLUTEN-FREE, ONE PAN

SERVES 4

PREP TIME:
15 minutes

COOK TIME:
15 minutes

The savory notes from the lamb and mushrooms make this a weekly comfort food staple. The family is happy because they always leave the table full; I'm happy because they walked away from the table with more fiber and vegetables than they agreed to.

3 thick lamb sausages, removed from casing and crumbled

1 medium shallot, chopped

1½ cups diced baby portobello mushrooms

1 teaspoon garlic powder

1 tablespoon extra-virgin olive oil

1 pound bean-based penne pasta

4 medium Roma tomatoes, chopped

1 (14.5-ounce) can crushed tomatoes

3 tablespoons heavy cream

1. Heat a large sauté pan or skillet over medium-high heat. Add the sausage to the skillet and cook for about 5 minutes, mixing and breaking the sausage up until the sausage is halfway cooked.

2. Reduce the heat to medium-low and add the shallot. Continue cooking for about 3 minutes, until they're soft. Add the mushrooms, garlic powder, and olive oil and cook for 5 to 7 minutes, until the mushrooms have reduced in size by half and all the water is cooked out.

3. Meanwhile, bring a large pot of water to a boil and cook the pasta according to the package directions, until al dente. Drain and set aside.

4. To the skillet, add the chopped and canned tomatoes and cook for 7 to 10 minutes, until the liquid thickens slightly. Reduce the heat and add the cream, mixing well.
5. Plate the pasta first and top with the sausage mixture.

SUBSTITUTION TIP: *If lamb isn't available, you can use lean ground beef.*

Per Serving Calories: 706; Protein: 45g; Total Carbohydrates: 79g; Sugars: 20g; Fiber: 18g; Total Fat: 31g; Saturated Fat: 10g; Cholesterol: 64mg; Sodium: 586mg

Marinated Lamb Kebabs with Crunchy Yogurt Dressing

SERVES 4

PREP TIME:
35 minutes

COOK TIME:
15 minutes

Lean cuts of lamb, such as sections of the leg, loin, and rack, are great options for your favorite recipes. Your most successful recipes will use dry-heat cooking methods to prepare these cuts, such as grilling, roasting, or broiling. Lamb can appear on a variety of seasonal menus and pairs with a diverse range of ingredients. If you are using wooden skewers, be sure to soak them for half an hour before using to prevent scorching.

½ cup plain, unsweetened, full-fat Greek yogurt

¼ cup extra-virgin olive oil

¼ cup freshly squeezed lemon juice

1 teaspoon grated lemon zest

2 garlic cloves, minced

2 tablespoons honey

2 tablespoons balsamic vinegar

1½ teaspoons oregano, fresh, minced

1 teaspoon thyme, fresh, minced

1 bay leaf

1 teaspoon kosher salt

½ teaspoon freshly ground black pepper

½ teaspoon red pepper flakes

2 pounds leg of lamb, trimmed, cleaned and cut into 1-inch pieces

1 large red onion, diced large

1 recipe Crunchy Yogurt Dip (page 190)

Parsley, chopped, for garnish

Lemon wedges, for garnish

1. In a bowl or large resealable bag, combine the yogurt, olive oil, lemon juice and zest, garlic, honey, balsamic vinegar, oregano, thyme, bay leaf, salt, pepper, and red pepper flakes. Mix well. Add the lamb pieces and marinate, refrigerated, for 30 minutes.
2. Preheat the oven to 375°F.

3. Thread the lamb onto the skewers, alternating with chunks of red onion as desired.
4. Put the skewers onto a baking sheet and roast for 10 to 15 minutes, rotating every 5 minutes to ensure that they cook evenly.
5. Plate the skewers and allow them to rest briefly.
6. Top or serve with the yogurt dressing.
7. To finish, garnish with fresh chopped parsley and a lemon wedge.

INGREDIENT TIP: *You can purchase lamb stew meat from many groceries as an alternative. However, for the best flavor and most tender cuts, use leg of lamb. See your local butcher or experienced grocery butcher in the meat department.*

LEFTOVER TIP: *Remove the lamb from the skewers and toss into your favorite salad for lunch the next day.*

RECIPE TIP: *These lamb skewers are great on the grill. Heat the grill to high. Place the skewers in the middle of the grill and reduce heat to medium-high. Close the grill and allow the skewers to cook for 10 to 15 minutes total, rotating every 2 minutes to ensure that they cook evenly.*

Per Serving Calories: 578; Protein: 56g; Total Carbohydrates: 20g; Sugars: 15g; Fiber: 1g; Total Fat: 30g; Saturated Fat: 9g; Cholesterol: 157mg; Sodium: 804mg

Garlic Pork Tenderloin and Lemony Orzo

30 MINUTES OR LESS, DAIRY-FREE, GLUTEN-FREE, ONE PAN

SERVES 6

PREP TIME:
15 minutes

COOK TIME:
20 minutes

Pork tenderloin is a delicious, tender, lean protein great for any day of the week. However, many chefs new to healthy cooking may have made tenderloin that ended up dry and inedible. If you remember to keep the cooking time to 20 minutes per pound, you should stay in the safe, delicious, juicy zone.

1 pound pork tenderloin

½ teaspoon Shawarma Spice Rub (page 162)

1 tablespoon salt

½ teaspoon coarsely ground black pepper

½ teaspoon garlic powder

6 tablespoons extra-virgin olive oil

3 cups Lemony Orzo (page 80)

1. Preheat the oven to 350°F.
2. Rub the pork with shawarma seasoning, salt, pepper, and garlic powder and drizzle with the olive oil.
3. Put the pork on a baking sheet and roast for 20 minutes, or until desired doneness.
4. Remove the pork from the oven and let rest for 10 minutes.
5. Assemble the pork on a plate with the orzo and enjoy.

INGREDIENT TIP: *Want to manage your own spices instead of purchasing a spice blend, like shawarma seasoning? Rub ⅛ teaspoon each of cumin, coriander, cardamom, and oregano into the pork.*

Per Serving Calories: 579; Protein: 33g; Total Carbohydrates: 37g; Sugars: 3g; Fiber: 3g; Total Fat: 34g; Saturated Fat: 9g; Cholesterol: 85mg; Sodium: 1,700mg

Roasted Pork with Apple-Dijon Sauce

GLUTEN-FREE

SERVES 8

PREP TIME:
15 minutes

COOK TIME:
40 minutes

The robust apple-Dijon sauce sets this dish apart from other pork tenderloin dinners. The mustard and apple undertones in the sauce remind me of a warm fall night.

1½ tablespoons
extra-virgin olive oil

1 (12-ounce)
pork tenderloin

¼ teaspoon kosher salt

¼ teaspoon freshly
ground black pepper

¼ cup apple jelly

¼ cup apple juice

2 to 3 tablespoons
Dijon mustard

½ tablespoon cornstarch

½ tablespoon cream

1. Preheat the oven to 325°F.
2. In a large sauté pan or skillet, heat the olive oil over medium heat.
3. Add the pork to the skillet, using tongs to turn and sear the pork on all sides. Once seared, sprinkle pork with salt and pepper, and set it on a small baking sheet.
4. In the same skillet, with the juices from the pork, mix the apple jelly, juice, and mustard into the pan juices. Heat thoroughly over low heat, stirring consistently for 5 minutes. Spoon over the pork.
5. Put the pork in the oven and roast for 15 to 17 minutes, or 20 minutes per pound. Every 10 to 15 minutes, baste the pork with the apple-mustard sauce.
6. Once the pork tenderloin is done, remove it from the oven and let it rest for 15 minutes. Then, cut it into 1-inch slices.
7. In a small pot, blend the cornstarch with cream. Heat over low heat. Add the pan juices into the pot, stirring for 2 minutes, until thickened. Serve the sauce over the pork.

Per Serving Calories: 146; Protein: 13g; Total Carbohydrates: 8g; Sugars: 5g; Fiber: 0g; Total Fat: 7g; Saturated Fat: 2g; Cholesterol: 35mg; Sodium: 192mg

Pressure Cooker Moroccan Pot Roast

DAIRY-FREE,
GLUTEN-FREE

SERVES 4

PREP TIME:
15 minutes

COOK TIME:
50 minutes

This quickly became a twice-monthly regular dinner. The leftovers make an absolutely delicious lunch the next day.

- 8 ounces mushrooms, sliced
- 4 tablespoons extra-virgin olive oil
- 3 small onions, cut into 2-inch pieces
- 2 tablespoons paprika
- 1½ tablespoons garam masala
- 2 teaspoons salt
- ¼ teaspoon ground white pepper
- 2 tablespoons tomato paste
- 1 small eggplant, peeled and diced
- 1¼ cups low-sodium beef broth
- ½ cup halved apricots
- ⅓ cup golden raisins
- 3 pounds beef chuck roast
- 2 tablespoons honey
- 1 tablespoon dried mint
- 2 cups cooked brown rice

1. Set an electric pressure cooker to Sauté and put the mushrooms and oil in the cooker. Sauté for 5 minutes, then add the onions, paprika, garam masala, salt, and white pepper. Stir in the tomato paste and continue to sauté.
2. Add the eggplant and sauté for 5 more minutes, until softened. Pour in the broth. Add the apricots and raisins. Sear the meat for 2 minutes on each side.
3. Close and lock the lid and set the pressure cooker to high for 50 minutes.
4. When cooking is complete, quick release the pressure. Carefully remove the lid, then remove the meat from the sauce and break it into pieces. While the meat is removed, stir honey and mint into the sauce.

5. Assemble plates with ½ cup of brown rice, ½ cup of pot roast sauce, and 3 to 5 pieces of pot roast.

VARIATION TIP: *Try cayenne or red pepper for extra heat. You can also add smoked paprika.*

Per Serving Calories: 829; Protein: 69g; Total Carbohydrates: 70g; Sugars: 33g; Fiber: 11g; Total Fat: 34g; Saturated Fat: 13g; Cholesterol: 275mg; Sodium: 1,556mg

Shawarma Pork Tenderloin with Pitas

DAIRY-FREE

SERVES 8

PREP TIME:
15 minutes

COOK TIME:
35 minutes

If you eat meat, you need this dish in your life. The shawarma spices transform this dish. The strong, savory herbs permeate the pork and bring you back into your favorite shawarma deli.

FOR THE SHAWARMA SPICE RUB

1 teaspoon ground cumin

1 teaspoon ground coriander

1 teaspoon ground turmeric

¾ teaspoon sweet Spanish paprika

½ teaspoon ground cloves

¼ teaspoon salt

¼ teaspoon freshly ground black pepper

⅛ teaspoon ground cinnamon

FOR THE SHAWARMA

1½ pounds pork tenderloin

3 tablespoons extra-virgin olive oil

1 tablespoon garlic powder

Salt

Freshly ground black pepper

1½ tablespoons Shawarma Spice Rub

4 pita pockets, halved, for serving

1 to 2 tomatoes, sliced, for serving

¼ cup Pickled Onions (page 188), for serving

¼ cup Pickled Turnips (page 187), for serving

¼ cup store-bought hummus or Garlic-Lemon Hummus (page 76)

TO MAKE THE SHAWARMA SEASONING

In a small bowl, combine the cumin, coriander, turmeric, paprika, cloves, salt, pepper, and cinnamon and set aside.

TO MAKE THE SHAWARMA

1. Preheat the oven to 400°F.
2. Put the pork tenderloin on a plate and cover with olive oil and garlic powder on each side. Season with salt and pepper and rub each side of the tenderloin with a generous amount of shawarma spices.
3. Place the pork tenderloin in the center of a roasting pan and roast for 20 minutes per pound, or until the meat begins to bounce back as you poke it. If it feels like there's still fluid under the skin, continue cooking. Check every 5 to 7 minutes until it reaches the desired tenderness and juices run clear.
4. Remove the pork from the oven and let rest for 10 minutes.
5. Serve the pork tenderloin shawarma with pita pockets, tomatoes, Pickled Onions (if using), Pickled Turnips (if using), and hummus.

INGREDIENT TIP: *If you undercook your pork, feel free to slice and panfry before eating.*

Per Serving Calories: 316; Protein: 29g; Total Carbohydrates: 17g; Sugars: 1g; Fiber: 3g; Total Fat: 15g; Saturated Fat: 3g; Cholesterol: 67mg; Sodium: 230mg

Flank Steak with Artichokes

**DAIRY-FREE,
GLUTEN-FREE**

SERVES
4 TO 6

PREP TIME:
15 minutes

COOK TIME:
60 minutes

I love how easily this dish lends itself to being eaten with couscous or rice. The juices created during the cooking process were made to be soaked up by crusty bread or rice.

4 tablespoons grapeseed oil, divided

2 pounds flank steak

1 (14-ounce) can artichoke hearts, drained and roughly chopped

1 onion, diced

8 garlic cloves, chopped

1 (32-ounce) container low-sodium beef broth

1 (14.5-ounce) can diced tomatoes, drained

1 cup tomato sauce

2 tablespoons tomato paste

1 teaspoon dried oregano

1 teaspoon dried parsley

1 teaspoon dried basil

½ teaspoon ground cumin

3 bay leaves

2 to 3 cups cooked couscous (optional)

1. Preheat the oven to 450°F.
2. In an oven-safe sauté pan or skillet, heat 3 tablespoons of oil on medium heat. Sear the steak for 2 minutes per side on both sides. Transfer the steak to the oven for 30 minutes, or until desired tenderness.
3. Meanwhile, in a large pot, combine the remaining 1 tablespoon of oil, artichoke hearts, onion, and garlic. Pour in the beef broth, tomatoes, tomato sauce, and tomato paste. Stir in oregano, parsley, basil, cumin, and bay leaves.
4. Cook the vegetables, covered, for 30 minutes. Remove bay leaf and serve with flank steak and ½ cup of couscous per plate, if using.

Per Serving Calories: 577; Protein: 55g; Total Carbohydrates: 22g; Sugars: 9g; Fiber: 6g; Total Fat: 28g; Saturated Fat: 1g; Cholesterol: 90mg; Sodium: 1,405mg

Easy Honey-Garlic Pork Chops

DAIRY-FREE, GLUTEN-FREE

SERVES 4

PREP TIME:
15 minutes

COOK TIME:
25 minutes

With a touch of sweet and sour, these pork chops offer a perfect combination. This is a stick-to-your-ribs dinner that you won't be able to stop eating.

4 pork chops, boneless or bone-in

¼ teaspoon salt

⅛ teaspoon freshly ground black pepper

3 tablespoons extra-virgin olive oil

5 tablespoons low-sodium chicken broth, divided

6 garlic cloves, minced

¼ cup honey

2 tablespoons apple cider vinegar

1. Season the pork chops with salt and pepper and set aside.
2. In a large sauté pan or skillet, heat the oil over medium-high heat. Add the pork chops and sear for 5 minutes on each side, or until golden brown.
3. Once the searing is complete, move the pork to a dish and reduce the skillet heat from medium-high to medium. Add 3 tablespoons of chicken broth to the pan; this will loosen the bits and flavors from the bottom of the skillet.
4. Once the broth has evaporated, add the garlic to the skillet and cook for 15 to 20 seconds, until fragrant. Add the honey, vinegar, and the remaining 2 tablespoons of broth. Bring the heat back up to medium-high and continue to cook for 3 to 4 minutes.
5. Stir periodically; the sauce is ready once it's thickened slightly. Add the pork chops back into the pan, cover them with the sauce, and cook for 2 minutes. Serve.

VARIATION TIP: *For a bit of heat to balance out the sweet, add in a dash of red pepper flakes.*

Per Serving Calories: 302; Protein: 22g; Total Carbohydrates: 19g; Sugars: 17g; Fiber: <1g; Total Fat: 16g; Saturated Fat: 4g; Cholesterol: 55mg; Sodium: 753mg

Moussaka

PREP TIME:
25 minutes

COOK TIME:
40 minutes

This traditional dish is a labor of love, and no Mediterranean cookbook would be complete without it. You will be fully rewarded for all the time and attention you poured into this dish the second you take your first bite.

FOR THE EGGPLANT

2 pounds eggplant, cut into ¼-inch-thick slices

1 teaspoon salt

2 to 3 tablespoons extra-virgin olive oil

FOR THE FILLING

1 tablespoon extra-virgin olive oil

2 shallots, diced

1 tablespoon dried, minced garlic

1 pound ground lamb

4 ounces portobello mushrooms, diced

1 (14.5-ounce) can crushed tomatoes, drained

¼ cup tomato paste

1 cup low-sodium beef broth

2 bay leaves

2 teaspoons dried oregano

¾ teaspoon salt

2½ cups store-bought béchamel sauce

⅓ cup panko bread crumbs

TO MAKE THE EGGPLANT

1. Preheat the oven to 450°F.
2. Line large baking sheets with paper towels and arrange the eggplant slices in a single layer and sprinkle with salt. Place another layer of paper towels on the eggplant slices. Continue until all eggplant slices are covered.
3. Let the eggplant sweat for 30 minutes to remove excess moisture. While this is happening, make the meat sauce.
4. Pat the eggplant dry. Dry the baking sheets and brush with oil and place the eggplant slices onto the baking sheets.
5. Bake for 15 to 20 minutes, or until lightly browned and softened. Remove from the oven and cool slightly before assembling the moussaka.

TO MAKE THE FILLING

1. In a large, oven-safe sauté pan or skillet, heat the olive oil over high heat. Cook the shallots and garlic for 2 minutes, until starting to soften.
2. Add the ground lamb and brown it with the garlic and onions, breaking it up as it cooks. Add the mushrooms and cook for 5 to 7 minutes, or until they have dehydrated slightly.
3. Add the tomatoes and paste, beef broth, bay leaves, oregano, and salt and stir to combine. Once the sauce is simmering, lower to medium-low and cook for 15 minutes, or until it reduces to a thick sauce. Remove the sauce to a separate bowl before assembly.
4. Reduce the oven temperature to 350°F.
5. Place half the eggplant slices in the bottom of the skillet used to make the sauce. Top the slices with all the meat filling.
6. Place the remaining eggplant on top of the meat filling and pour the jarred béchamel sauce over the eggplant. Sprinkle with the bread crumbs.
7. Bake for 30 to 40 minutes or until golden brown. Let stand for 10 minutes before serving.

SUBSTITUTION TIP: *Swap out the ground lamb for ground turkey to make this dish a bit lighter.*

Per Serving Calories: 491; Protein: 23g; Total Carbohydrates: 30g; Sugars: 14g; Fiber: 6g; Total Fat: 33g; Saturated Fat: 14g; Cholesterol: 83mg; Sodium: 1,522mg

Shortbread with Strawberry Preserves, page 176

Sweets and Desserts

Baklava

VEGETARIAN

SERVES 12

PREP TIME:
10 minutes

COOK TIME:
40 minutes

This is the easiest dessert you never knew you could make. It's dangerous how easy (and drop-dead delicious) this dessert is. The cinnamon flavors the walnuts and both play off the buttery pastry sheets and sweet, sticky honey.

1½ cups finely chopped walnuts

1 teaspoon ground cinnamon

¼ teaspoon ground cardamom (optional)

1 cup water

½ cup sugar

½ cup honey

2 tablespoons freshly squeezed lemon juice

1 cup salted butter, melted

20 large sheets phyllo pastry dough, at room temperature

1. Preheat the oven to 350°F.
2. In a small bowl, gently mix the walnuts, cinnamon, and cardamom (if using) and set aside.
3. In a small pot, bring the water, sugar, honey, and lemon juice just to a boil. Remove from the heat.
4. Put the butter in a small bowl. Onto an ungreased 9-by-13-inch baking sheet, put 1 layer of phyllo dough and slowly brush with butter. Be careful not to tear the phyllo sheets as you butter them. Carefully layer 1 or 2 more phyllo sheets, brushing each with butter in the baking pan, and then layer ⅛ of the nut mix; layer 2 sheets and add another ⅛ of the nut mix; repeat with 2 sheets and nuts until you run out of nuts and dough, topping with the remaining phyllo dough sheets.
5. Slice 4 lines into the baklava lengthwise and make another 4 or 5 slices diagonally across the pan.

6. Put in the oven and cook for 30 to 40 minutes, or until golden brown.
7. Remove the baklava from the oven and immediately cover it with the syrup.

INGREDIENT TIP: *Leave the baklava out as long as possible before storing any leftovers. This dish tends to get soggy once it's wrapped up.*

Per Serving Calories: 443; Protein: 6g; Total Carbohydrates: 47g; Sugars: 22g; Fiber: 3g; Total Fat: 27g; Saturated Fat: 11g; Cholesterol: 41mg; Sodium: 344mg

Lemon Cookies

30 MINUTES OR LESS, VEGETARIAN

SERVES 12 COOKIES

PREP TIME:
10 minutes

COOK TIME:
10 minutes

This recipe was given to me by one of my first (and closest) friends in Colorado. We first made it in her ranch kitchen in northern Denver. They ended up being our dessert every night that weekend.

Nonstick cooking spray

¾ cup granulated sugar

½ cup butter

1½ teaspoons vinegar

1 large egg

1 teaspoon grated lemon zest

1¾ cup flour

1 teaspoon baking powder

¼ teaspoon baking soda

¾ cup confectioners' sugar

¼ cup freshly squeezed lemon juice

1 teaspoon finely grated lemon zest

1. Preheat the oven to 350°F. Spray a baking sheet with cooking spray and set aside.
2. In a medium bowl, cream the sugar and butter. Next, stir in the vinegar, and then add the egg and lemon zest, and mix well. Sift the flour, baking powder, and baking soda into the bowl and mix until combined.
3. Spoon the mixture onto a prepared baking sheet in 12 equal heaps. Bake for 10 to 12 minutes. Be sure not to burn the bottoms.
4. While the cookies are baking, make the lemon glaze in a small bowl by mixing the sugar, lemon juice, and lemon zest together.
5. Remove the cookies from the oven and brush with lemon glaze.

VARIATION TIP: *Try this recipe with almond milk or orange zest for a different flavor profile.*

Per Serving Calories: 233; Protein: 3g; Total Carbohydrates: 39g; Sugars: 26g; Fiber: 1g; Total Fat: 8g; Saturated Fat: 5g; Cholesterol: 37mg; Sodium: 132mg

Vanilla Bites

VEGETARIAN

MAKES 24 BITES

PREP TIME:
10 minutes

COOK TIME:
45 minutes

These little bites pack a flavor punch. You'll have to double and triple your batches after the first time you make them.

1 (12-ounce) box butter cake mix

½ cup (1 stick) butter, melted

3 large eggs, divided

1 cup sugar

1 (8-ounce) cream cheese

1 teaspoon vanilla extract

1. Preheat the oven to 350°F.
2. To make the first layer, in a medium bowl, blend the cake mix, butter, and 1 egg. Then, pour the mixture into the prepared pan.
3. In a separate bowl, to make layer 2, mix together sugar, cream cheese, the remaining 2 eggs, and vanilla and pour this gently over the first layer. Bake for 45 to 50 minutes and allow to cool.
4. Cut the cake into 24 small squares.

RECIPE TIP: *For a reduced-fat version, try reduced-fat cream cheese.*

STORAGE TIP: *Store in an airtight container in the refrigerator for 5 to 7 days.*

Per Serving Calories: 160; Protein: 2g; Total Carbohydrates: 20g; Sugars: 15g; Fiber: 0g; Total Fat: 8g; Saturated Fat: 5g; Cholesterol: 44mg; Sodium: 156mg

Cranberry Loaf Roll-Up

VEGETARIAN

PREP TIME:
20 minutes,
plus
90 minutes
inactive time

COOK TIME:
45 minutes

This roll-up loaf is too good to be limited by titles. No one was upset about this loaf seeing daylight at our regular Sunday brunch; we even have requests for a second appearance next month.

FOR THE DOUGH

3 cups all-purpose flour

1 (0.25-ounce) package quick-rise yeast

½ teaspoon salt

⅛ teaspoon ground cinnamon

⅛ teaspoon ground cardamom

½ cup water

½ cup almond milk

⅓ cup butter, cubed

FOR THE CRANBERRY FILLING

1 (12-ounce) can cranberry sauce

½ cup chopped walnuts

2 tablespoons grated orange zest

2 tablespoons orange juice

1. In a large bowl, combine the flour, yeast, salt, cinnamon, and cardamom.
2. In a small pot, heat the water, almond milk, and butter over medium-high heat. Once it boils, reduce the heat to medium-low. Simmer for 10 to 15 minutes, until the liquid thickens.
3. Pour the liquid ingredients into the dry ingredients and, using a wooden spoon or spatula, mix the dough until it forms a ball in the bowl.
4. Put the dough in a greased bowl, cover tightly with a kitchen towel, and set aside for 1 hour.
5. **To make the cranberry filling:** In a medium bowl, mix the cranberry sauce with walnuts, orange zest, and orange juice in a large bowl.

TO ASSEMBLE THE BREAD

1. Roll out the dough to about a 1-inch-thick and 10-by-7-inch-wide rectangle.
2. Spread the cranberry filling evenly on the surface of the rolled-out dough, leaving a 1-inch border around the edges. Starting with the long side, tuck the dough under with your fingertips and roll up the dough tightly. Place the rolled-up dough in an "S" shape in a bread pan.
3. Allow the bread to rise again, about 30 to 40 minutes.
4. Preheat the oven to 350°F.
5. Bake in a preheated oven, 45 minutes.

SUBSTITUTION TIP: *If you don't have almond milk, you can try fat-free cow's milk.*

Per Serving (4 servings) Calories: 704; Protein: 12g;
Total Carbohydrates: 111g; Sugars: 35g; Fiber: 6g; Total Fat: 26g;
Saturated Fat: 11g; Cholesterol: 41mg; Sodium: 448mg

Shortbread with Strawberry Preserves

30 MINUTES OR LESS, VEGETARIAN

MAKES 3 DOZEN COOKIES

PREP TIME:
20 minutes

COOK TIME:
10 minutes

My sister first showed me how to make this recipe, teaching me how to knead it without overworking it while her kids were running in and out of the kitchen. Overworking doughs tends to yield a dense and tough cookie.

2 cups cornstarch

1½ cups all-purpose flour

2 teaspoons baking powder

1 teaspoon baking soda

1 cup (2 sticks) cold butter, cut into 1-inch cubes

⅔ cup sugar

4 large egg yolks

2 tablespoons brandy

1 teaspoon vanilla extract

½ teaspoon salt

2 cups strawberry preserves

Confectioners' sugar, for sprinkling

1. In a bowl, combine the cornstarch, flour, baking powder, and baking soda and mix together. Using your hands or 2 forks, mix the butter and sugar just until combined, with small pieces of butter remaining.
2. Add the egg yolks, brandy, vanilla, and salt, stirring slowly until all ingredients are blended together. If you have a stand mixer, you can mix these ingredients together with the paddle attachment and then finish mixing by hand, but it is not required.
3. Wrap the dough in plastic wrap and place in a resealable plastic bag for at least 1 hour.
4. Preheat the oven to 350°F.
5. Roll the dough to ¼-inch thickness and cut, placing 12 cookies on a sheet. Bake the sheets one at a time on the top rack of the oven for 12 to 14 minutes.

6. Let the cookies cool completely and top with about 1 tablespoon of strawberry preserves.
7. Sprinkle with confectioners' sugar.

INGREDIENT TIP: *This is a dry, crumbly dough. Work it a bit with your hands before adding additional egg yolks. The dough should be whitish, almost chalky-looking. If it looks more yellowish and is too easy to work with, there is too much egg and some cornstarch or flour should be added.*

VARIATION TIP: *Roll the sides with coconut flakes.*

Per Serving Calories: 157; Protein: 1g; Total Carbohydrates: 26g; Sugars: 12g; Fiber: <1g; Total Fat: 6g; Saturated Fat: 3g; Cholesterol: 34mg; Sodium: 132mg

Citrus Pound Cake

VEGETARIAN

SERVES 8

PREP TIME:
10 minutes

COOK TIME:
45 minutes

This cake is the perfect midweek pick-me-up. Its light and flavorful body makes for a great snack after lunch or a decadent dessert with a glass of Chianti.

FOR THE CAKE
Nonstick cooking spray

1 cup sugar

⅓ cup extra-virgin olive oil

1 cup buttermilk

1 lemon, zested and juiced

2 cups all-purpose flour

1 teaspoon baking soda

1 teaspoon salt

FOR THE GLAZE
1 cup powdered sugar

1 to 2 tablespoons freshly squeezed lemon juice

½ teaspoon vanilla extract

TO MAKE THE CAKE

1. Preheat the oven to 350°F. Line a 9-inch loaf pan with parchment paper and coat the paper with nonstick cooking spray.
2. In a large bowl, whisk together the sugar and olive oil until creamy. Whisk in the buttermilk and lemon juice and zest. Let it stand for 5 to 7 minutes.
3. In a medium bowl, combine the flour, baking soda, and salt. Fold the dry ingredients into the buttermilk mixture and stir just until incorporated.
4. Pour the batter into the prepared pan and smooth the top. Bake until a toothpick or skewer inserted into the middle comes out clean with a few crumbs attached, about 45 minutes.
5. Remove the cake from the oven and cool for at least 10 minutes in the pan. Transfer to a cooling rack placed over a baking sheet and cool completely.

TO MAKE THE GLAZE

In a small bowl, whisk together the powdered sugar, lemon juice, and vanilla until smooth. Pour the glaze over the cooled cake, allowing the excess to drip off the cake onto the baking sheet beneath.

VARIATION TIP: *Try switching up the glaze flavors. Blood-orange extract and a couple tablespoons of fresh orange juice in place of lemon juice heightens this dish's flavor in a refreshing and exciting way.*

Per Serving Calories: 347; Protein: 4g; Total Carbohydrates: 64g; Sugars: 41g; Fiber: 1g; Total Fat: 9g; Saturated Fat: 1g; Cholesterol: 1mg; Sodium: 481mg

Individual Apple Pockets

30 MINUTES OR LESS, VEGETARIAN

SERVES 6

PREP TIME:
5 minutes

COOK TIME:
15 minutes

This is one dessert that I don't feel guilty about going back for third or fourth helpings. You can see the melted brown sugar and cinnamon glistening on the apple slices in each pocket.

1 organic puff pastry, rolled out, at room temperature

1 Gala apple, peeled and sliced

¼ cup brown sugar

⅛ teaspoon ground cinnamon

⅛ teaspoon ground cardamom

Nonstick cooking spray

Honey, for topping

1. Preheat the oven to 350°F.
2. Cut the pastry dough into 4 even discs. Peel and slice the apple. In a small bowl, toss the slices with brown sugar, cinnamon, and cardamom.
3. Spray a muffin tin very well with nonstick cooking spray. Be sure to spray only the muffin holders you plan to use.
4. Once sprayed, line the bottom of the muffin tin with the dough and place 1 or 2 broken apple slices on top. Fold the remaining dough over the apple and drizzle with honey.
5. Bake for 15 minutes or until brown and bubbly.

VARIATION TIP: *For a gluten-free version of this dessert, use gluten-free puff pastry, which can be found online or at some grocery stores.*

Per Serving Calories: 250; Protein: 3g; Total Carbohydrates: 30g; Sugars: 9g; Fiber: 1g; Total Fat: 15g; Saturated Fat: 2g; Cholesterol: 0mg; Sodium: 98mg

Avocado-Orange Fruit Salad

30 MINUTES OR LESS, DAIRY-FREE, GLUTEN-FREE, VEGETARIAN

SERVES 5 TO 6

PREP TIME:
10 minutes

This no-fuss dessert reminds me of family Christmas gatherings. We would always have this in the dessert spread, as the healthier dessert, to go with the lemon cookies.

2 large Gala apples, chopped

2 oranges, segmented and chopped

⅓ cup sliced almonds

½ cup honey

1 tablespoon extra-virgin olive oil

½ teaspoon grated orange zest

1 large avocado, semi-ripened, medium diced

1. In a large bowl, combine the apples, oranges, and almonds. Mix gently.
2. In a small bowl, whisk the honey, oil, and orange zest. Set aside.
3. Drizzle the orange zest mix over the fruit salad and toss. Add the avocado and toss gently one more time.

VARIATION TIP: *Swap in berries and sliced pears for the apples.*

Per Serving Calories: 296; Protein: 3g; Total Carbohydrates: 51g; Sugars: 42g; Fiber: 7g; Total Fat: 12g; Saturated Fat: 1g; Cholesterol: 0mg; Sodium: 4mg

CLOCKWISE FROM TOP LEFT:
Berry and Honey Compote,
page 189; Sweet Red Wine
Vinaigrette, page 185; Tzatziki
Sauce, page 192; Pickled Onions,
page 188; Spicy Cucumber
Dressing, page 191

Sauces, Dips, and Dressings

Herbed Oil

30 MINUTES OR LESS, DAIRY-FREE, GLUTEN-FREE, VEGAN

SERVES 2

PREP TIME: 5 minutes

This is the oil plate you always hope to see waiting for you next to a basket of freshly baked table bread. For some heat, sprinkle in some red pepper flakes.

½ cup extra-virgin olive oil

1 teaspoon dried basil

1 teaspoon dried parsley

1 teaspoon fresh rosemary leaves

2 teaspoons dried oregano

⅛ teaspoon salt

Pour the oil into a small bowl and stir in the basil, parsley, rosemary, oregano, and salt while whisking the oil with a fork.

STORAGE TIP: *Make the herbed oil up to 2 days in advance; keep refrigerated.*

INGREDIENT TIP: *Fresh herbs will work just as well as dried in this dish. I recommend doubling the amount of fresh herbs versus their dried counterparts because fresh herbs have a milder flavor.*

Per Serving Calories: 486; Protein: 1g; Total Carbohydrates: 2g; Sugars: <1g; Fiber: 1g; Total Fat: 54g; Saturated Fat: 7g; Cholesterol: 0mg; Sodium: 78mg

Sweet Red Wine Vinaigrette

30 MINUTES OR LESS, GLUTEN-FREE

SERVES 2

PREP TIME:
5 minutes

It's hard to go wrong with red wine vinegar. It's a classic and versatile vinegar; the one drawback is its strong taste. If you want to try this with less of a vinegar bite, try using solely apple cider vinegar.

¼ cup plus 2 tablespoons extra-virgin olive oil

2 tablespoons red wine vinegar

1 tablespoon apple cider vinegar

2 teaspoons honey

2 teaspoons Dijon mustard

½ teaspoon minced garlic

⅛ teaspoon kosher salt

⅛ teaspoon freshly ground black pepper

In a jar, combine the olive oil, vinegars, honey, mustard, garlic, salt, and pepper and shake well.

STORAGE TIP: *Store in an airtight container for 1 to 2 days.*

VARIATION TIP: *Try this dressing with some added orange zest for a new twist.*

Per Serving Calories: 386; Protein: <1g; Total Carbohydrates: 6g; Sugars: 6g; Fiber: 0g; Total Fat: 41g; Saturated Fat: 6g; Cholesterol: 0mg; Sodium: 198mg

Skinny Cider Dressing

30 MINUTES OR LESS, DAIRY-FREE, GLUTEN-FREE, VEGAN

SERVES 2

PREP TIME:
5 minutes

Clean and simple, this dressing has only a few ingredients but bold taste. For stronger lemon flavor, add the juice of an additional half of a lemon to the dressing.

2 tablespoons apple cider vinegar

⅓ lemon, juiced

⅓ lemon, zested

Salt

Freshly ground black pepper

In a jar, combine the vinegar, lemon juice, and zest. Season with salt and pepper, cover, and shake well.

STORAGE TIP: *Store in an airtight container for 1 to 2 days.*

VARIATION TIP: *If you don't have apple cider vinegar, try red wine vinegar instead.*

Per Serving Calories: 2; Protein: 0g; Total Carbohydrates: 1g; Sugars: <1g; Fiber: <1g; Total Fat: 0g; Saturated Fat: 0g; Cholesterol: 0mg; Sodium: <1mg

Pickled Turnips

30 MINUTES OR LESS, DAIRY-FREE, GLUTEN-FREE, VEGAN

MAKES ABOUT 1 QUART

PREP TIME: 5 minutes

The dried Turkish oregano makes this pickling savory. Check your local produce areas for prewashed and precut produce to cut down on cleaning, peeling, and slicing.

1 pound turnips, washed well, peeled, and cut into 1-inch batons

1 small beet, roasted, peeled, and cut into 1-inch batons

2 garlic cloves, smashed

1 teaspoon dried Turkish oregano

3 cups warm water

½ cup red wine vinegar

½ cup white vinegar

In a jar, combine the turnips, beet, garlic, and oregano. Pour the water and vinegars over the vegetables, cover, then shake well and put it in the refrigerator. The turnips will be pickled after 1 hour.

INGREDIENT TIP: *Try to select gluten-free vinegars (most vinegars other than malts) to keep this dish free of gluten.*

STORAGE TIP: *You may store the turnips for up to 2 weeks in a refrigerated, airtight container.*

Per Serving (1 to 2 tablespoons) Calories: 3; Protein: <1g; Total Carbohydrates: 1g; Sugars: <1g; Fiber: <1g; Total Fat: 0g; Saturated Fat: 0g; Cholesterol: 0mg; Sodium: 6mg

Pickled Onions

30 MINUTES OR LESS, DAIRY-FREE, GLUTEN-FREE, VEGAN

SERVES 8 TO 10

PREP TIME: 5 minutes

I picked up this recipe when my dad lived in Mexico City. A friend's mother shared it with me while showing me how to make homemade tortillas. The homemade tortillas are another story, but these pickled onions are good on anything. Sandwiches, burgers, pitas, wraps—my husband and I have tried them all and have been happier for it.

3 red onions, finely chopped

½ cup warm water

¼ cup granulated sugar

¼ cup red wine vinegar

1 teaspoon dried oregano

In a jar, combine the onions, water, sugar, vinegar, and oregano, then shake well and put it in the refrigerator. The onions will be pickled after 1 hour.

VARIATION TIP: *Add carrots to this jar for a delicious new crunch to your pitas or salads.*

STORAGE TIP: *Store the onions for up to 2 weeks, refrigerated, in an airtight container.*

Per Serving Calories: 40; Protein: 1g; Total Carbohydrates: 10g; Sugars: 8g; Fiber: 1g; Total Fat: <1g; Saturated Fat: 0g; Cholesterol: 0mg; Sodium: 1mg

Berry and Honey Compote

**30 MINUTES
OR LESS,
DAIRY-FREE,
GLUTEN-FREE,
VEGETARIAN**

**SERVES
2 TO 3**

PREP TIME:
5 minutes

COOK TIME:
15 seconds

This is the missing ingredient for your favorite breakfast dish. I remember making this with my mom when, on a busy Sunday brunch day, we realized there was no syrup. Needless to say, we stopped looking for syrup after we threw this new brunch staple together.

½ **cup honey**

¼ **cup fresh berries**

2 **tablespoons grated orange zest**

In a small saucepan, heat the honey, berries, and orange zest over medium-low heat for 2 to 5 minutes, until the sauce thickens, or heat for 15 seconds in the microwave. Serve the compote drizzled over pancakes, muffins, or French toast.

STORAGE TIP: *Store in an airtight jar in the refrigerator, but this compote is best enjoyed the same day it's made.*

VARIATION TIP: *If you don't have an orange, you can try this dish citrus-free or with grapefruit zest.*

Per Serving Calories: 272; Protein: 1g; Total Carbohydrates: 74g; Sugars: 71g; Fiber: 1g; Total Fat: <1g; Saturated Fat: 0g; Cholesterol: 0mg; Sodium: 4mg

Crunchy Yogurt Dip

30 MINUTES OR LESS, GLUTEN-FREE, VEGETARIAN

SERVES 2 TO 3

PREP TIME: 5 minutes

The crunch from this dip comes from the cucumber's refreshing and strong, yet subtle, flavor. This dip makes a great addition to any appetizer spread.

1 cup plain, unsweetened, full-fat Greek yogurt

½ cup cucumber, peeled, seeded, and diced

1 tablespoon freshly squeezed lemon juice

1 tablespoon chopped fresh mint

1 small garlic clove, minced

Salt

Freshly ground black pepper

1. In a food processor, combine the yogurt, cucumber, lemon juice, mint, and garlic. Pulse several times to combine, leaving noticeable cucumber chunks.
2. Taste and season with salt and pepper.

STORAGE TIP: *Store in an airtight container for 1 to 2 days.*

SUBSTITUTION TIP: *If you don't have Greek yogurt, try reduced-fat or fat-free sour cream.*

Per Serving Calories: 128; Protein: 11g; Total Carbohydrates: 7g; Sugars: 6g; Fiber: <1g; Total Fat: 6g; Saturated Fat: 3g; Cholesterol: 16mg; Sodium: 47mg

Spicy Cucumber Dressing

30 MINUTES OR LESS, GLUTEN-FREE, VEGETARIAN

SERVES 2

PREP TIME:
5 minutes

The spicy profile of this dish comes from the garlic. If you want to dial up the heat (and push away any nearby family members), add another tablespoon of minced garlic into the dressing.

1½ cups plain, unsweetened, full-fat Greek yogurt

1 cucumber, seeded and peeled

½ lemon, juiced and zested

1 tablespoon dried, minced garlic

½ tablespoon dried dill

2 teaspoons dried oregano

Salt

In a food processor, combine the yogurt, cucumber, lemon juice, garlic, dill, oregano, and a pinch of salt and process until smooth. Adjust the seasonings as needed and transfer to a serving bowl.

STORAGE TIP: *Store in an airtight container for 1 to 2 days.*

VARIATION TIP: *For added heat, stir up to an additional 2 tablespoons dried garlic and/or ⅛ teaspoon white pepper into the dressing.*

Per Serving Calories: 209; Protein: 18g; Total Carbohydrates: 14g; Sugars: 9g; Fiber: 2g; Total Fat: 10g; Saturated Fat: 5g; Cholesterol: 24mg; Sodium: 69mg

Tzatziki Sauce

GLUTEN-FREE, VEGETARIAN

SERVES 2

PREP TIME:
5 minutes

The dill and cucumbers make a dynamic combination in this sauce. I use this as a topping for tilapia, grilled chicken breasts, and sandwiches (instead of mayonnaise), or as a dip for sliced vegetables.

1 medium cucumber, peeled, seeded and diced

½ teaspoon salt, divided, plus more

½ cup plain, unsweetened, full-fat Greek yogurt

½ lemon, juiced

1 tablespoon chopped fresh parsley

½ teaspoon dried minced garlic

½ teaspoon dried dill

Freshly ground black pepper

1. Put the cucumber in a colander. Sprinkle with ¼ teaspoon of salt and toss. Let the cucumber rest at room temperature in the colander for 30 minutes.
2. Rinse the cucumber in cool water and place in a single layer on several layers of paper towels to remove the excess liquid.
3. In a food processor, pulse the cucumber to chop finely and drain off any extra fluid.
4. Pour the cucumber into a mixing bowl and add the yogurt, lemon juice, parsley, garlic, dill, and the remaining ¼ teaspoon of salt. Season with salt and pepper to taste and whisk the ingredients together. Refrigerate in an airtight container.

INGREDIENT TIP: *If cucumber causes you to have reflux, try finding hothouse, burpless cucumbers. Also, be mindful to extract all the seeds out of the cucumber, as they tend to worsen symptoms.*

STORAGE TIP: *Place in an airtight container for 1 to 2 days.*

Per Serving Calories: 77; Protein: 6g; Total Carbohydrates: 6g; Sugars: 4g; Fiber: 1g; Total Fat: 3g; Saturated Fat: 2g; Cholesterol: 8mg; Sodium: 607mg

Citrus Garlic Dressing

30 MINUTES OR LESS, GLUTEN-FREE, VEGAN

SERVES 2

PREP TIME:
5 minutes

This dressing has kept salads interesting. I can make this on Sunday night and have enough for lunch salads until Thursday. I usually like to add the orange I zested and juiced into the salad I'm using the dressing on; it highlights the orange notes in the dressing.

¼ cup extra-virgin olive oil

2 tablespoons freshly squeezed orange juice

1 orange, zested

1 teaspoon garlic powder

¾ teaspoon za'atar seasoning

½ teaspoon salt

¼ teaspoon Dijon mustard

Freshly ground black pepper

In a jar, combine the olive oil, orange juice and zest, garlic powder, za'atar, salt, and mustard. Season with pepper and shake vigorously until completely mixed.

SUBSTITUTION TIP: *Don't have za'atar? Use dried oregano.*

STORAGE TIP: *Keep in a mason jar (or old tomato sauce jar) for up to 4 days.*

Per Serving Calories: 283; Protein: 1g; Total Carbohydrates: 11g; Sugars: 8g; Fiber: 2g; Total Fat: 27g; Saturated Fat: 4g; Cholesterol: 0mg; Sodium: 597mg

Cider Yogurt Dressing

30 MINUTES OR LESS, GLUTEN-FREE, VEGETARIAN

SERVES 3

PREP TIME:
5 minutes

The yogurt makes this a substantial dressing. The higher-fat yogurt creates a better finished product. I usually try to find the highest-fat plain Greek yogurt available when making this dressing.

1 cup plain, unsweetened, full-fat Greek yogurt

½ cup extra-virgin olive oil

1 tablespoon apple cider vinegar

½ lemon, juiced

1 tablespoon chopped fresh oregano

½ teaspoon dried parsley

½ teaspoon kosher salt

¼ teaspoon garlic powder

¼ teaspoon freshly ground black pepper

In a large bowl, combine the yogurt, olive oil, vinegar, lemon juice, oregano, parsley, salt, garlic powder, and pepper and whisk well.

INGREDIENT TIP: *I like to use 5-percent-fat Greek yogurt, but if you can't find it, try to get the highest fat content you can. Fat is an important macronutrient that offers a smoother, more satiating dish.*

STORAGE TIP: *Use immediately or refrigerate for up to 1 week, shaking to emulsify again before use.*

Per Serving Calories: 402; Protein: 8g; Total Carbohydrates: 4g; Sugars: 4g; Fiber: <1g; Total Fat: 40g; Saturated Fat: 7g; Cholesterol: 11mg; Sodium: 417mg

Creamy Citrus Dressing

30 MINUTES OR LESS, GLUTEN-FREE, VEGETARIAN

SERVES 2

PREP TIME:
5 minutes

The creamy, full-fat Greek yogurt and bright lemon notes play off each other well in this dressing.

1 cup plain, unsweetened, full-fat Greek yogurt

1 large lemon, zested and juiced

½ teaspoon dried oregano

½ teaspoon dried parsley

1½ teaspoons garlic salt

Freshly ground black pepper

In a medium bowl, whisk the yogurt, lemon juice and zest, oregano, parsley, and garlic salt. Season with pepper. Pour over the salad of your choice.

VARIATION TIP: *If you want, try this recipe with mandarin oranges. It'll create a tart and sweet flavor profile.*

STORAGE TIP: *Store in an airtight container for no longer than 2 days.*

Per Serving Calories: 133; Protein: 11g; Total Carbohydrates: 10g; Sugars: 6g; Fiber: 1g; Total Fat: 6g; Saturated Fat: 3g; Cholesterol: 16mg; Sodium: 1,093mg

MEASUREMENT CONVERSIONS

VOLUME EQUIVALENTS (LIQUID)

US STANDARD	US STANDARD (OUNCES)	METRIC (APPROXIMATE)
2 tablespoons	1 fl. oz.	30 mL
¼ cup	2 fl. oz.	60 mL
½ cup	4 fl. oz.	120 mL
1 cup	8 fl. oz.	240 mL
1½ cups	12 fl. oz.	355 mL
2 cups or 1 pint	16 fl. oz.	475 mL
4 cups or 1 quart	32 fl. oz.	1 L
1 gallon	128 fl. oz.	4 L

OVEN TEMPERATURES

FAHRENHEIT (F)	CELSIUS (C) (APPROXIMATE)
250°F	120°C
300°F	150°C
325°F	165°C
350°F	180°C
375°F	190°C
400°F	200°C
425°F	220°C
450°F	230°C

VOLUME EQUIVALENTS (DRY)

US STANDARD	METRIC (APPROXIMATE)
⅛ teaspoon	0.5 mL
¼ teaspoon	1 mL
½ teaspoon	2 mL
¾ teaspoon	4 mL
1 teaspoon	5 mL
1 tablespoon	15 mL
¼ cup	59 mL
⅓ cup	79 mL
½ cup	118 mL
⅔ cup	156 mL
¾ cup	177 mL
1 cup	235 mL
2 cups or 1 pint	475 mL
3 cups	700 mL
4 cups or 1 quart	1 L

WEIGHT EQUIVALENTS

US STANDARD	METRIC (APPROXIMATE)
½ ounce	15 g
1 ounce	30 g
2 ounces	60 g
4 ounces	115 g
8 ounces	225 g
12 ounces	340 g
16 ounces or 1 pound	455 g

REFERENCES

Buettner, D., and S. Skemp. "Blue Zones, Lessons From the World's Longest Lived." *American Journal of Lifestyle Medicine* 10, no. 5 (July 2016): 318–321. doi.org /10.1177/1559827616637066.

Dohrmann, D. D., P. Putnik, D. Bursać Kovačević, J. Simal-Gandara, J. M. Lorenzo, and F. J. Barba. "Japanese, Mediterranean and Argentinean Diets and Their Potential Roles in Neurodegenerative Diseases." *Food Research International* 120 (June 2019): 464–477. doi.org/10.1016/j.foodres.2018.10.090.

Estruch, R., E. Ros, J. Salas-Salvado, M. I. Covas, D. Corella, F. Arós, E. Gómez-Gracia, V. Ruiz-Gutiérrez, M. Fiol, J. Lapetra, R. M. Lamuela-Raventos, L. Serra-Majem, X. Pintó, J. Basora, M. A. Muñoz, J. V. Sorlí, J. A. Martínez, M. Fitó, A. Gea, M. A. Hernán, and M. A. Martínez-González. "Primary Prevention of Cardiovascular Disease with a Mediterranean Diet Supplemented with Extra-Virgin Olive Oil or Nuts." *New England Journal of Medicine* 378, no. 25 (June 21, 2018*):* e34. doi.org/10.1056 /NEJMoa1800389.

Lăcătușu, C. M., E. D. Grigorescu, M. Floria, A. Onofriescu, and B. M. Mihai. "The Mediterranean Diet: From an Environment-Driven Food Culture to an Emerging Medical Prescription" *International Journal of Environmental Research and Public Health* 16, no. 6 (March 2019). doi.org/10.3390/ijerph16060942.

Tosti V., B. Bertozzi, and L. Fontana. "Health Benefits of the Mediterranean Diet: Metabolic and Molecular Mechanisms." *Journal of Gerontology, Series A, Biological Sciences and Medical Sciences* 73, no. 3 (March 2018): 318–326.

INDEX

ABOUT THE AUTHOR

As a Registered Dietitian and Certified Diabetes Educator, I've had the privilege of spending the last 10 years of my career helping individuals manage their diseases and lose weight while eating what they love and finding peace with food.

Working one-on-one with clients for so many years has given me a unique understanding of what individuals struggle with and what resources they need in order to be successful in achieving their goals. I believe in simple, sustainable, and results-driven strategies when it comes to nutrition. Through this approach, clients reach lasting nutrition success.

In good health,

CHRISTINE PATORNITI, RD, CDE, MBA
REGISTERED DIETITIAN, CERTIFIED DIABETES EDUCATOR
NUTRITION CENTER OF COLORADO, LLC